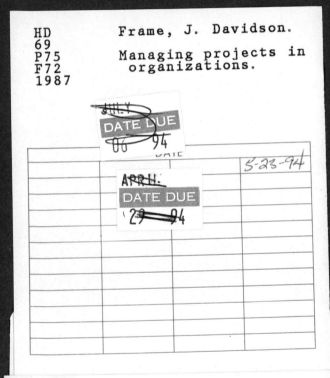

Managing Projects
in Organizations

J. Davidson Frame

Managing Projects
in Organizations

How to Make the Best Use of Time, Techniques, and People

Jossey-Bass Publishers

San Francisco   •   Oxford   •   1991

MANAGING PROJECTS IN ORGANIZATIONS
How to Make the Best Use of Time, Techniques, and People
by J. Davidson Frame

Copyright © 1987 by: Jossey-Bass Inc., Publishers
350 Sansome Street
San Francisco, California 94104
&
Jossey-Bass Limited
Headington Hill Hall
Oxford OX3 0BW

Library of Congress Cataloging-in-Publication Data

Frame, J. Davidson.
  Managing projects in organizations.

  (The Jossey-Bass management series)
  Bibliography: p. 231
  Includes index.
  1. Industrial project management. I. Title.
II. Series.
HD69.P75F72   1987   658.4'04   86-33707
ISBN 1-55542-031-1 (alk. paper)

Manufactured in the United States of America

The paper in this book meets the guidelines for
permanence and durability of the Committee on
Production Guidelines for Book Longevity of the
Council on Library Resources.

JACKET DESIGN BY WILLI BAUM

FIRST EDITION

HB Printing   10 9 8 7 6

Code 8709

The Jossey-Bass
Management Series

Contents

To Katherine and Nancy

Preface

This book is written for information-age workers searching for a way to get a handle on the projects they have been assigned to run. I am talking here about office workers, educators, information systems managers, R & D personnel, lawyers, writers, budgeters, and the vast number of other people whose work causes them to manipulate information rather than tangible things. It is likely that these individuals have drifted into positions of responsibility as a natural outgrowth of their routine activities. By showing some degree of initiative and organizational ability in carrying out their daily tasks, they find one day that they have been given responsibility for carrying out a project.

Project management has been called the accidental profession. It is accidental in at least two senses. First, it is not a profession that people consciously choose to pursue. No child answers the question ''What do you want to be when you grow up?'' with the answer ''Why, a project manager, of course.'' People typically become project managers after stumbling onto project management responsibilities.

Project management is an accidental profession in a second sense as well: knowledge of how to run projects is not acquired through systematic inquiry but is gained in a hit-or-miss fashion. Having received little or no formal preparation for their jobs, typical project managers set out to reinvent the fundamental precepts of project management. Frequently their trial-

and-error efforts result in costly mistakes. If novice project managers are good at their jobs, they chalk up these mistakes to experience and avoid them in the future. After five to ten years of this process, the novice (if he or she has survived this long) graduates to the status of seasoned professional.

A partial exception to this state of affairs is found in the construction, defense, and allied industries. In these areas, project management methodologies have been developed and applied over several decades, and project staff are often systematically trained in their use. As a consequence, we find an abundant literature that provides guidance for project managers in the construction and defense industries.

Parallel guidance for information-age project workers is scarce. Unfortunately, a good deal of the material developed for the construction and defense industries is only marginally relevant to information-age projects. One problem is that construction and defense projects focus on concrete things (hardware), whereas information-age projects deal more with intangibles (software, in the broadest sense of the word). Another is that construction and defense projects tend to be large, costly, highly structured efforts that must be approached formally, whereas the information-age projects carried out by white-collar professionals tend to be smaller and much more flexible.

I have worked with information-age projects all my adult life. As an undergraduate and graduate student, I was continuously immersed in information-based projects—homework assignments, computer programming, term papers, and doctoral dissertation. In industry, I was a full-time project manager for seven years, running about twenty-five archetypical information-age projects. Most of them involved the design of scientific research evaluation systems, software development, office automation, and the writing of technical reports. Like 99 percent of my colleagues, I learned project management on the job. In 1979, I left industry for academia, and since then I have been teaching graduate courses on project management.

During the past few years, I have also been conducting four-day seminars on the management of information-age projects, focusing on nonhardware projects. About a thousand experienced project managers have taken the seminar. My family refers to these seminars as my road show, since they are held in different cities throughout the United States. In the summer of 1985 and throughout the autumn of 1986, I carried my road show to China, where I lectured extensively on project management for the Chinese Academy of Science. It was comforting to see that Murphy's law is as alive in China as in the United States.

My experiences both as a practicing project manager and a teacher have led me to conclude that what information-age project managers want and need is a practical and flexible approach to managing their projects. This book is designed to give them such an approach. It recognizes that many of the commonly employed tools used on traditional projects are of limited utility to information-age knowledge workers. It shows how, with some modification, the traditional tools can be usefully employed on these projects. It also offers insights into new tools that are just now emerging and are ideally suited for application on information-age projects.

Chapter One provides a broad overview of what project management is about. Terms are defined, and the different stages of the project life cycle are described. Special attention focuses on two key lessons that the book emphasizes: avoiding pitfalls and making things happen.

The next two chapters focus on projects in their organizational context. Chapter Two examines how organizational issues can lead to project success or failure. One of the principal organizational realities that project managers face is lack of authority to control directly the resources necessary for carrying out a project. Another is the central importance of politics in projects. Chapter Two offers strategies for coping with these and additional organizational realities.

Chapter Three shows how project managers can improve their managerial efficacy by paying more attention to the people involved in projects. The most difficult aspect of project management is the management of human resources. When managers develop a knack for dealing with project staff, bosses, vendors, and fellow managers who control needed resources, they increase immeasurably the likelihood of project success.

The relationship between team structure and effective project management is the topic of Chapter Four. A major goal of good project managers is to fashion effective teams in environments that are inherently inimical to team building. This chapter offers pointers on how managers can improve the chances of a project's success by selecting a team structure that enhances team efficiency. Special attention is directed to four team structures that seem particularly effective in projects: isomorphic, speciality, egoless, and surgical teams.

While Chapters Two through Four focus on projects from the perspective of organizational issues, Chapters Five and Six cast light on the interrelated topics of needs and requirements analysis. While everyone acknowledges that cost and schedule overruns are bad, a little reflection suggests that the most serious failing a project can have is to produce a deliverable that is not utilized or is underutilized or misutilized. If we define project failure in this way, then it becomes clear that an enormous fraction of the projects we undertake are in some sense failures.

An examination of why project deliverables are not utilized, or are underutilized or misutilized, suggests that the source of the problem is that end-user needs have not been met or that the requirements defining the deliverable are poorly specified. Chapter Five offers ways to improve identification of end-user needs (for example, by building a needs hierarchy), while Chapter Six provides suggestions on defining requirements more effectively (for example, by employing the recently developed application prototyping methodology).

Chapters Seven and Eight look at a third pitfall in the management of projects: poor planning and control. Chapter Seven describes the standard tools used for enhancing planning and control—for example, work breakdown structures, Gantt charts, PERT/CPM networks, resource loading charts, and resource spreadsheets. Chapter Eight discusses special planning and control topics that are not usually covered in conventional project management texts: planning and control of multiple-project portfolios, very large projects, and projects that are carried out under contract. Planning and control tools that are infrequently discussed—such as the earned value approach, gap analysis, and the bureaucratic milestone review technique—are investigated here.

Finally, Chapter Nine brings together the different pieces into a cohesive whole.

Good tools make our jobs as project managers easier, but the tools by themselves will not assure success—or even mediocre performance. Going beyond a mere litany of project management techniques, the book offers an overall methodology for dealing with information-age projects. It emphasizes seeing projects in their organizational context. It stresses doing things right at the earliest stages of a project's evolution in order to minimize the inevitable grief of having to do things over again later.

When projects are carried out nicely, and chaos is converted into order, project managers justifiably feel as high as kites, denizens of a heaven of sorts that is reserved for the super competent. When projects go wrong, they can be like hell on earth. I hope that this book will help project managers affix the wings that will enable them to reach the heights. But as experienced project managers, we are always looking over our shoulders, always aware of the ever present law of Murphy. Let's aim for the heights . . . but remember Icarus, remember Lucifer.

There are many people whom I would like to thank for helping to make this book possible. Norma Maine Loeser and Erik Winslow, both of the School of Government and Business Administration at George Washington University, provided me with important material and moral support. Peter Zuckerman, of the U.S. Professional Development Institute, helped me launch the road show that brought me into contact with hundreds of project managers, whose stories and insights underlie practically every page of this book. William Wells of George Washington University, whom I affectionately refer to as my partner in crime, spent many hours scheming with me to come up with better ways to teach project management courses. Nancy Frame, an accomplished project manager in her own right, read and criticized my manuscript as it evolved. Finally, five-year-old Katherine Frame walked on her tiptoes each time she passed my office and would resist for a few brief moments the temptation to exercise to its fullest the natural exuberance that is so much a part of her.

Washington, D.C.   J. Davidson Frame
January 1987

The Author

J. Davidson Frame is professor of management science at the School of Government and Business Administration, George Washington University, Washington, D.C. He teaches graduate courses on the management of technology, project management, and statistics and, from 1982 to 1986, was director of the Program on Science, Technology, and Innovation. Frame has a B.A. degree (1967) from the College of Wooster in history and M.A. (1969) and Ph.D. (1976) degrees from the American University in international relations, focusing primarily on econometrics and economic development.

Prior to entering academia, Frame was vice-president of Computer Horizons, Inc., and manager of its Washington office. While at Computer Horizons, he managed some twenty-five information-age projects.

In addition to teaching graduate-level project management courses, Frame travels throughout the United States and abroad, offering a four-day project management seminar. More than a thousand project managers have attended this seminar.

Frame's project management research has focused on quantitative approaches to selecting and evaluating technical projects. He has written more than thirty scholarly articles, twenty technical reports, chapters in several books, and a book entitled *International Business and Global Technology* (1983).

Managing Projects
in Organizations

Understanding the Process
of Managing Projects

Projects have been with us for a very long time. People have been undertaking them since the earliest days of organized human activity. The hunting parties of our prehistoric forebears were projects, for example; they were temporary undertakings directed at the goal of obtaining meat for the community. Large, complex projects have also been with us for a long time. The pyramids, the Great Wall of China, and Hadrian's Wall were projects that, in their time, were of roughly the same dimensions as the Manhattan Project to build an atomic bomb or the Apollo project to send men to the moon.

All of us are constantly undertaking projects in our day-to-day lives. Some common examples are preparing for a picnic, repairing the leaky faucet, fixing up the house for Aunt Telia's visit, and writing a term paper for school. Projects are an integral part of our lives. Typically, we carry out these projects in a haphazard way. We finally get around to fixing the faucet when we can no longer tolerate the din of dripping water, and we begin writing our term paper the day before it is due. We tell a subordinate in an offhand manner to develop a marketing plan, and we are upset with him when the completed plan in no way looks like what we envisioned. We are given money to investigate the physical properties of a new polymer, but we run out of cash before we are even half finished with our work.

We are surrounded by projects, we work on them daily, but rarely do we consciously strive to get a grip on them—to *manage* them. Although people have been carrying out projects for millennia, project management as a unique management form is a recent development. To a large degree, it was a by-product of the major projects of World War II, the best known being the Manhattan Project. A conscious attempt was made to coordinate the enormous budget, schedule, and resource complexity of the Manhattan Project in as efficient a way as possible. Management of the Manhattan Project moved project management from the realm of the accidental to the domain—at least ideally—of the carefully contrived.

In the past few years, project management has become a hot management approach. As the United States economy has entered a postindustrial phase, American managers have discovered that many of the management guidelines established for a manufacturing economy no longer serve them well in an information economy. In a manufacturing environment, emphasis is placed on predictability and repetitive activities, and management is to a large extent concerned with standardization and rationalization of production processes.

With an information economy, uniqueness of events has replaced repetition. Information itself is dynamic and ever changing. Flexibility is the watchword of the new order, and project management is a key to this flexibility.

What Is a Project?

We use the term *project* frequently in our daily conversations. A husband, for example, tells his wife, "My main project for this weekend is to straighten out the garage." Going hunting, building pyramids, fixing faucets, and preparing for a picnic share a number of common features that make them projects:

- They are goal-oriented.
- They involve the coordinated undertaking of interrelated activities.
- They are of finite duration, with beginnings and ends.

- They are each, to a degree, unique.

   In general, these four characteristics distinguish projects from other undertakings. Each of these characteristics has important implications, so we should examine them closely.

   Goal-Orientation. Projects are directed at achieving specific results—that is, they are goal-oriented. It is these goals that drive the project, and all planning and implementation efforts are undertaken so as to achieve them.

   Projects are permeated with goals from top to bottom. The principal goal of a computer software project may be to develop a sophisticated data base management system. An intermediate goal will be to test the evolving system to free it from bugs, while a lower-level goal will be to identify days when project staff are available to attend progress meetings.

   The fact that projects are goal-oriented carries with it enormous implications for their management. For one thing, it suggests that an important feature of managing projects is to identify relevant goals, starting at the highest level and then working down to the grass roots. It also suggests that a project can be viewed as the pursuit of carefully chosen goals and that progress on the project entails achieving ever higher levels of goals, until finally we have attained the ultimate goal.

   Fortunately for those of us concerned with managing projects, a whole methodology has been developed over the last few decades to help us in setting and achieving goals. This methodology is called *management by objectives* (MBO), and its development occurred independently of the growth of project management. A solid grasp of the basic principles of MBO can make a project manager's life easier.

   Coordinated Undertaking of Interrelated Activities. Projects are inherently complex. They entail carrying out multiple activities that are related to each other in both obvious and subtle ways. Some tasks cannot be executed until other tasks have been completed, some must be carried out in parallel, and so on. Should the tasks get out of sync with each other, the whole project may be jeopardized.

If we reflect awhile upon this characteristic of projects, we realize that a project is a system—that is, a whole made up of interrelated parts. Once again, the project manager is in luck: as in the case of MBO, management specialists have over the last few decades developed sophisticated methodologies for dealing with systems. These methodologies taken together are called *systems analysis*. The project manager who has a grasp of the basic principles of systems analysis can use that knowledge to great effect in running projects.

Limited Duration. Projects are undertaken in a finite period of time (although to project managers facing schedule slippages, it may seem as if projects endure an eternity). They are temporary. They have reasonably well-defined beginnings and ends. When the basic project goals are achieved, the project ends. A large part of the project effort is dedicated to ensuring that the project is completed at the appointed time. To do this, schedules are created showing when tasks should begin and end.

Contrast this to typical production runs for successful manufactured products. The product is cranked out indefinitely, depending upon how much demand there is for it. When demand disappears, the production run ceases. Production runs are not projects.

Uniqueness. Projects are to a degree nonrecurring, one-of-a-kind undertakings. However, the extent of uniqueness varies considerably from project to project. If you are an engineer building the fiftieth identical ranch-style unit in a housing tract, the extent of uniqueness is quite low. The basic elements of this house are identical to those in the forty-nine other houses you have built. The principal sources of uniqueness may lie in the special soil conditions surrounding the house, the requirement to install a new model boiler for the first time, the need to work with a new team of carpenters, and so forth.

On the other hand, if you are designing the operating system of a fifth-generation computer, you are clearly working on a highly unique effort. You are doing something that has not been done before. Because past experiences offer you little precise guidance on what you can expect in your project, it is filled with risk and uncertainty.

What Is Project Management?

If you ask seasoned project managers to describe their most fundamental objective in carrying out a project, you are likely to hear the following response: "To get the job done!" This is the project manager's universal credo. If project managers are given a few moments to reflect further upon their efforts, they will probably amplify their response as follows: "My most basic objective is to get the job done—*on time, within budget,* and *according to specifications.*"

These three items are so commonly identified by project managers as important parameters in the project management process that they have been given a name: the triple constraint. They constitute the focal point of the project manager's attention and energy. Project management entails carrying out a project as effectively as possible in respect to the constraints of time, money (and the resources it buys), and specifications.

Over the years, an array of tools have been developed to help project managers cope with the triple constraint.

In order to deal with the time constraint, project managers establish deadlines and work with schedules. Some fairly sophisticated computer-assisted scheduling tools—such as PERT/CPM, GERT, and VERT—are at the disposal of project managers to help them manage the time dimension more effectively.

Money constraints are handled with budgets. First, estimates are made as to what the project tasks will cost. Once the project is under way, the budget is monitored to see whether costs are getting out of hand.

Money buys resources, and project managers have developed several tools for managing human and material resources: for example, resource loading charts, resource Gantt charts, and linear responsibility charts.

Of the three basic constraints, the most difficult to manage is specifications. Specifications describe what the product of our project effort should look like. For example, if we are building a boat, one specification we might have to address is that the boat be 5.23 meters long. If we are designing a word processing system, we might have to wrestle with a specification requiring that the system be learnable by secretaries receiving only three days of training.

The problem with specifications is that they are notoriously difficult to establish and monitor. We will look at this issue in some detail in this book. For the moment, let it be noted that project managers have been struggling mightily to come up with techniques for developing and monitoring specifications, without too much success.

The Project Life Cycle

Projects have beginnings, middle periods, and endings. This may seem like a self-evident point, but it is not trivial if you are concerned with the management of projects, since where you are in the project life cycle will have a strong bearing on what you should be doing and what options are open to you.

There are many different ways in which project managers view the project life cycle. One of the most common has the life cycle broken into four broad phases: project conception, planning, implementation, and termination. In the information sciences, one often-used approach to the life cycle focuses on the following phases: needs recognition, requirements definition, system design, implementation, testing, and maintenance. Figures 1.1a and 1.1b provide a graphical approach to the project life cycle. They show that during their lifetimes projects consume varying levels of resources (for example, money, people, materials). In Figure 1.1a, the project gears up quickly and then slowly winds down. This could illustrate a typical market research project, where there is a lot of front-end activity such as gathering consumer data through questionnaires and interviews. Once the data are gathered, resource consumption drops off gradually as data are analyzed and findings are written up. In Figure 1.1b, we encounter a gradual build-up of activity until the project peaks, and then we have a rapid end. This often occurs with scientific research projects, where substantial time may be devoted to establishing research hypotheses, designing an experiment, setting up equipment, and so forth. Project activity reaches a peak when the experiment is actually carried out and the resulting data are observed.

Figure 1.1. The Project Life Cycle.

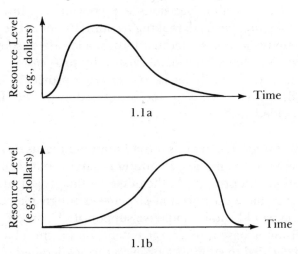

1.1a

1.1b

Regardless of the specific approach to the life cycle one takes, the main point to bear in mind is that over their lives projects are dynamic, continuously evolving organisms.

One approach that usefully illustrates the chief features of the life cycle disaggregates the cycle into six functions that are addressed during the course of a project: project selection, planning, implementation, control, evaluation, and termination. Let's briefly examine each of the six functions.

Project Selection. Projects arise out of needs. The whole project management process begins when someone somewhere has a need to be fulfilled. The need may be to reduce the number of forms that patients have to fill out in a hospital admissions procedure, or to develop antisatellite weapons, or to throw a party for little Katy's fifth birthday. Unfortunately, we live in a world of resource scarcity, and we cannot develop projects to address all of our needs. Choices have be made.

With project selection, we make our choices. We select some projects and reject others. Decisions are made on the basis of how many resources are available to us, how many different needs must be addressed, the cost of fulfilling those needs, and the relative importance of satisfying one set of needs and ignoring others.

Project selection decisions are enormously important, because they involve us in making a commitment to the future. They tie up resources, sometimes for just a few days, sometimes for years. They have what economists refer to as *opportunity costs* associated with them. That is, by selecting project A and not project B, we are giving up the benefits that project B could have provided us.

Planning. The plan is a road map, telling us how to get from one point to another. Planning is carried out throughout the duration of a project. At the outset of the project life cycle, we typically have an informal *pre*plan—a rough idea of what the project would entail should we support it. The project selection decision is based, to a large extent, on this preplan. Once we have decided to support a project, formal detailed planning commences. Project milestones are identified, and tasks and their interdependencies are laid out. A plethora of tools exist to assist the project manager in devising the formal project plan: work-breakdown structures, Gantt charts, network diagrams, resource allocation charts, resource loading charts, linear responsibility charts, cumulative cost distributions, and so forth.

As the project is carried out, the plan may undergo continual modification, reflecting encounters with and responses to unanticipated circumstances. Project plans are rarely static statements of how things should be done; instead, they are dynamic instruments, allowing project staff to manage change in an orderly fashion.

Implementation. When a formal plan has been devised, we are ready to carry out the project. Military personnel like to call this process project execution, but this term has an air of finality about it that may make the typical project manager a little nervous. When you have your head on the block, as many project managers do, you don't want to hear any talk about execution! So we use the term *implementation* here.

In a sense, implementation lies at the heart of a project, since it entails our doing the things that need to be done—as spelled out in the project plan—in order to produce something to meet the users' needs.

Precisely how the project is implemented is dependent upon its specific nature. In a construction project, foundations are poured, scaffolding is erected, and so on. In a drug development project, new compounds are tested in a laboratory and then clinically tested. In a market research project, customer attitudes are measured by means of questionnaires and interviews.

Control. As the project is being implemented, project managers continually monitor progress. They look at what has been done on the project, they look at the plan, and they determine whether there are major discrepancies between the two. In project management, these discrepancies are called *variances.* Unfortunately, one absolute certainty in project management is that there *will* be variances. We have not yet mastered forecasting to the point where we have a precise idea of what the future holds, and so long as the future is clouded with uncertainty, our project plans will be imperfect. In controlling a project, then, the question is not "Do we have variances?" Rather, it is "Are the variances we have acceptably small?"

The acceptable levels of variance should be determined at the outset of the project. In a typical construction project, acceptable levels are low, because the building contractor has a good deal of experience in building houses and knows what it takes to do the job. In addition, houses are usually built on a fixed-price basis (that is, the contractors agree ahead of time to sell their services for a given price). If cost variances are too great and they incur major cost overruns, building contractors will lose money on their projects. Consequently, there is great incentive to keep variances low.

In a speculative research project, acceptable variances may be quite high—say, in the range of 20 percent. Because research usually entails substantial uncertainty, the research plan is necessarily crude. We have only the roughest idea of how things will turn out, so we must be willing to accept wide divergences from our initial expectations.

The collection and examination of data on a project's progress lies at the center of the control process. Given this information, project managers have various courses of action they can pursue. For example, if their schedule is slipping unacceptably, they may decide to speed up a number of critical tasks by devoting more resources to them. If they find that for one series of tasks their staff have spent 40 percent less than planned, they will want to investigate this variance, since the underspending suggests that work is not being done or that corners are being cut.

Evaluation. Like control, evaluation serves an important feedback function. There are, however, a number of significant differences between evaluation and control.

- Control entails continual monitoring of project progress, while evaluation involves periodic stock-taking.
- Control focuses on the details of what is occurring in the project, whereas evaluation is more concerned with the big picture.
- Control activities are the responsibility of the project manager, while evaluations are typically carried out by an individual or group not directly working on the project (so as to maintain objectivity).

These practical distinctions between evaluation and control suggest the following nonrigorous definition of evaluation: evaluation is an objective, periodic stock-taking to determine the status of a project in relation to its specified goals.

Evaluations occur in midproject and also at the end of the project. Clearly, the basic role of evaluation is different in these two instances. With midproject evaluation, we can use the results of our findings to affect the future course of the project. In fact, the consequences of midproject evaluation can be dramatic—a premature termination of the project, a reassess-

Figure 1.2. Major Consequences of Midproject Evaluation.

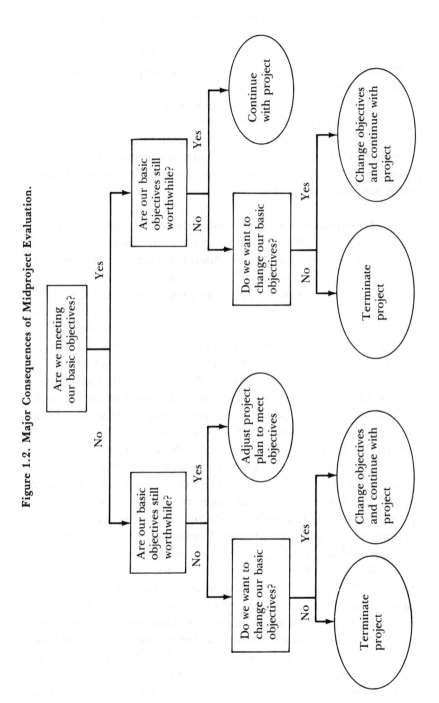

grammers, integrators, and testers collaborate to produce instructions that will cause electronic devices to perform miracles. Software development has become very important in our information-age economy and will continue to grow in importance in the future. It is interesting to note that software workers over the past one to two decades have created their own approaches to the management of software projects and that their approaches are largely independent of the traditional project management approaches. For example, the well-known structured techniques (structured design, structured programming, structured walk-throughs) owe no debt to traditional project management thinking.

In this book, I take special note of the management requirements of information-age projects. These are projects carried out by office workers, educators, information systems managers, R & D personnel, lawyers, writers, budgeters, and other people whose work causes them to manipulate information rather than tangible things. Liberal use is made of cases and examples of their work. I also offer examples from the construction and defense industries, even though this is not an engineering project management book. I typically use these examples to illustrate the contrast between the classical, well-structured project environment and the amorphous, free-flow environment facing today's information-age workers.

Key Lessons to Learn

A project manager is something like the driver of a car, the windshield spattered with an opaque layer of mud, who is trying to negotiate the vehicle down a steep, twisting road filled with potholes and littered with broken shards of glass, boulders, and patches of treacherous ice. It is a hazardous undertaking.

This book can be viewed as a travel guide written to help project managers negotiate their difficult journey. It is in part a road map, designed to guide project managers over the twists and turns of the contorted course. A special feature of this road map is that it points out the more salient obstacles project managers are likely to encounter on the way. It is also a repair guide, giving project managers pointers on preventive mainte-

Figure 1.2. Major Consequences of Midproject Evaluation.

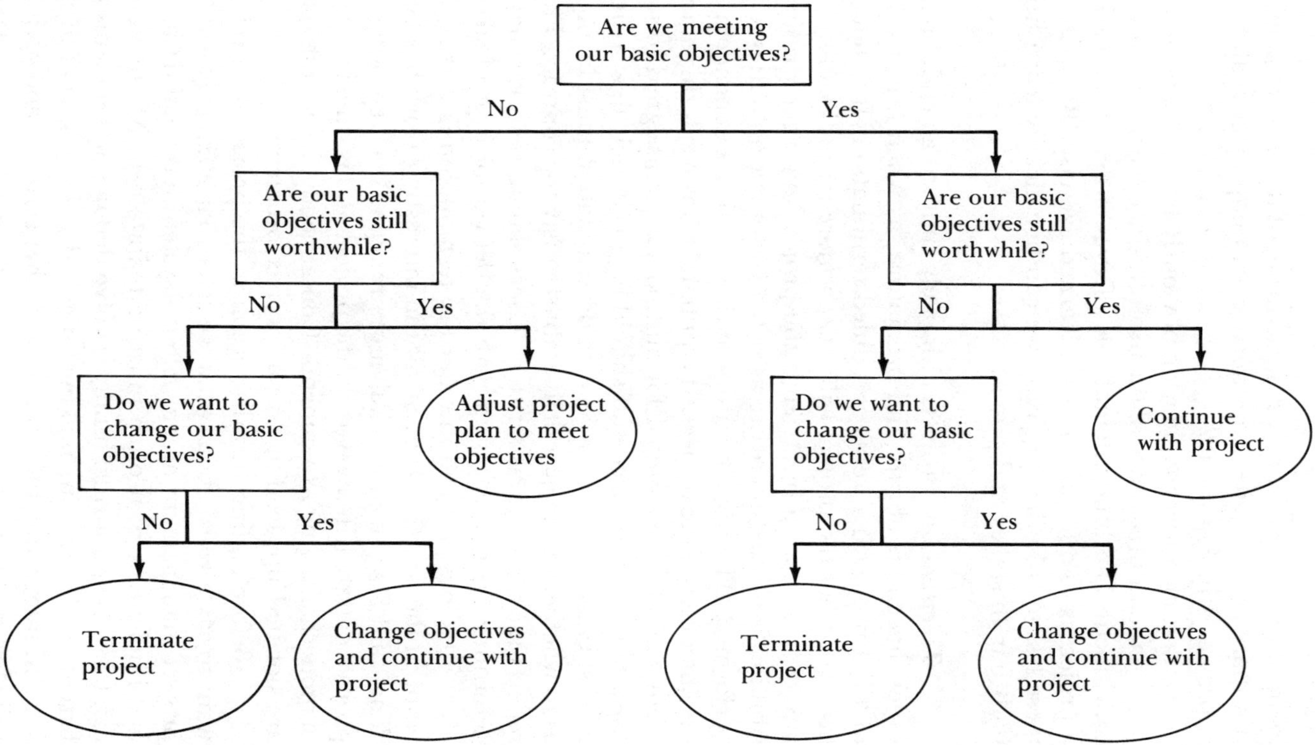

ment of project goals, or a restructuring of the project plan. A summary of the major consequences of midproject evaluation is provided in Figure 1.2.

End-of-project evaluation obviously will not have an impact on the future course of the project, since the project is now concluded. The fundamental role of evaluation at the end of a project is to offer us a lessons-learned exercise. By applying these lessons to other projects, we can beneficially learn from both our mistakes and our successes.

Termination. Projects ultimately come to an end. Sometimes this end is abrupt and premature, as when it is decided to kill a project before its scheduled termination. It is hoped, however, that the project will meet a more natural ending. In any event, when projects end, the project manager's responsibilities continue; there are assorted wrapping-up duties to be performed. The precise nature of these duties is dependent on the character of the project. If equipment was used, this equipment should be accounted for and possibly reassigned to new uses. Similarly, project staff should be given their new assignments. On contracted projects, a determination must be made as to whether the project deliverables satisfy the contract. Final reports may have to be written. Users should be contacted to determine their satisfaction with the deliverables. And so on.

One big problem in regard to termination is that at this point in the project life cycle all the interesting work has been done, and few—if any—challenges remain. It is tempting for project staff to drift away from the project at this time in search of more challenging assignments. Consequently, loose ends often are not tied up, leading to postproject problems.

Before ending this discussion of the project life cycle, I want to say a word about what we refer to as *maintenance* in the project management arena. After a system has been designed and implemented, it often must be maintained. Maintenance can take several forms: it may involve debugging problems inherent in the system, making so-called enhancements to the system, integrating the system with other systems, and periodically testing the system to determine whether it is still performing the way it should be. Systems maintenance is very important. It has been estimated, for example, that roughly 60 to 70 percent of the life cycle cost of computer systems is devoted to maintenance!

Although I believe that maintenance is crucially important, I do not include it in the project life cycle for a good reason. Projects, it should be recalled, are efforts that occur within a finite period of time. They have clearly defined beginnings and ends. Maintenance, on the other hand, is ongoing and of an indefinite duration. A specific act of maintenance—for example, revision of corporate purchasing guidelines—may be viewed as a project, but it is a separate and distinct undertaking from the initial project that produced the original guidelines.

Project Management in the Information Age

Project management has traditionally been carried out in the construction, architecture, and engineering professions, where there has been a need to get a firm handle on large, complex undertakings. Most of the tools used in project management evolved in an environment where men and women build things—and fairly large things at that!

In the past two or three decades, we have been dramatically propelled into an age where people are working less with tangible things and more with intangible information. This is reflected in statistics that show that some three-fourths of the American working population is engaged in service sector jobs, many of which involve the manipulation of information.

Because knowledge workers function heavily in the realm of the intangible, the character of their projects is fundamentally different from what one finds in, say, the construction industry. For example, they operate in a fuzzy world where it is often difficult to define precisely what they are supposed to do and how they are to go about doing it. Consequently, many of the project management tools developed for working with tangibles are of marginal use to them.

The archetypical information-age project involves computer software development. Systems architects, analysts, programmers, integrators, and testers collaborate to produce instructions that will cause electronic devices to perform miracles. Software development has become very important in our information-age economy and will continue to grow in importance in the future. It is interesting to note that software workers over the past one to two decades have created their own approaches to the management of software projects and that their approaches are largely independent of the traditional project management approaches. For example, the well-known structured techniques (structured design, structured programming, structured walkthroughs) owe no debt to traditional project management thinking.

In this book, I take special note of the management requirements of information-age projects. These are projects carried out by office workers, educators, information systems managers, R & D personnel, lawyers, writers, budgeters, and other people whose work causes them to manipulate information rather than tangible things. Liberal use is made of cases and examples of their work. I also offer examples from the construction and defense industries, even though this is not an engineering project management book. I typically use these examples to illustrate the contrast between the classical, well-structured project environment and the amorphous, free-flow environment facing today's information-age workers.

Key Lessons to Learn

A project manager is something like the driver of a car, the windshield spattered with an opaque layer of mud, who is trying to negotiate the vehicle down a steep, twisting road filled with potholes and littered with broken shards of glass, boulders, and patches of treacherous ice. It is a hazardous undertaking.

This book can be viewed as a travel guide written to help project managers negotiate their difficult journey. It is in part a road map, designed to guide project managers over the twists and turns of the contorted course. A special feature of this road map is that it points out the more salient obstacles project managers are likely to encounter on the way. It is also a repair guide, giving project managers pointers on preventive maintenance (so that they can avoid serious breakdowns), and showing them how to make minor repairs when needed.

Managing projects is difficult. The environment in which projects are carried out is complex. Common wisdom has it that the only certainty governing project performance is Murphy's law—if something can go wrong, it will go wrong. The inherent difficulty of managing projects is exacerbated by the fact that people typically stumble into project management responsibilities with no systematic project management training, giving rise to the observation that project management is the accidental profession.

While it is naive to suppose that managing projects can be made easy, it needn't be as difficult as many project managers make it. Effective project management can be learned. There are two fundamental lessons that the effective project manager masters. One is how to identify and avoid some of the common pitfalls encountered in managing projects. With this knowledge, the project manager can avoid the more obvious potholes and obstacles. The second lesson is how to organize and carry out the project for success—how to make things happen. It is not enough simply to avoid problems. The effective project manager must also proactively guide the project forward in the best manner possible.

The primary goal of this book is to convey these two lessons to the reader.

Lesson 1: Avoiding Pitfalls

Things *will* go wrong on projects. Of this the project manager can be sure. Perfectionists who are running their first project will be plagued with disappointment, for despite their best efforts at planning and controlling project activities, they will find that things never go precisely as expected; and if they are hell-bent on sticking with their original plan because of their belief that it is perfect, they are going to face serious troubles.

The major goal of effective project managers is not to design the perfect project, but rather to recognize that problems *will* arise in spite of their best efforts and to minimize the negative consequences of these unanticipated problems. Projects are filled with pitfalls, and as we shall see in the following chapters, many are not of the project manager's making. Yet project managers must deal with them. If they cannot do so effectively, their projects will fail in some sense: they may face unmanageable budget overruns, damaging schedule slippages, reductions in quality of the product they are developing, or worse. Effective project managers must anticipate the pitfalls they will encounter and, having done this, figure out ways to avoid them.

There are many ways in which projects can go awry. Generally, though, there are three principal sources of project failure. First, projects fail because of *organizational factors.* Second, they often fail because *user needs have been poorly identified and project requirements have been inadequately specified.* Third, they commonly fail because of *poor planning and control.* Let's look more closely at each of these factors.

Organizational Factors. It has been said that from an aerodynamic standpoint the bumblebee should not be able to fly. When we look at the organizational setting in which projects are carried out, we might similarly be tempted to say that it should be impossible to undertake projects effectively.

Most project managers are aware that many of the problems they face are tied to organizational issues. That is, they sense that arbitrary work rules, micromanagement from the top ranks of the hierarchy, the inability to get the right people for the job, haphazard budgeting, and so forth, make a tough job a lot tougher than necessary. What is interesting is that these project managers seem to believe that the organizational problems they face are unique to their particular organization. They harbor the notion that things are better outside of their own particular environment. They do not realize that many of the organizational problems they face are ubiquitous. *These problems are the norm:* the very nature of project management assures that they will arise.

To illustrate this, consider one common characteristic of project management: project managers rarely have direct control over much of anything. They are given responsibility to carry out the project (that is, heads will roll if things go wrong), but little or no authority to ensure that things will be done in precisely the way they desire. Let us look for a moment at a project manager responsible for carrying out an office relocation project for a company that will be moving to larger quarters in a modern building in a different city. Who will comprise her staff? She may be given a full-time assistant to help her out for the duration of the project. Chances are, however, that this assistant will be on temporary loan to her. When the project ends, the assistant will return to regular duties elsewhere in the organization. This project manager may work with an architect for several weeks in order to design the layout of the new facilities; but, once again, the architect is not her employee. She will also work with an interior decorator who will help her select appropriate furnishings for the new location, with a moving company, with building maintenance personnel, with higher levels of management in her company, and so forth. She has little or no direct control over these people, however, though they are vital to the success of the project.

For the most part, this is the way things have to be, since it would not be cost-effective to have an architect, interior decorator, and moving company worker permanently assigned to the project. Because of these circumstances, the project manager has little direct authority to impose her will on the individuals working on the project. If the project is to succeed, it will largely be a consequence of her ability to *coordinate* and *influence* the relevant project actors—and the willingness of these actors to cooperate with her.

The organizational factors discussed here require certain qualities in effective project managers. These managers should first of all be aware of the limitations of the job; they should recognize that as project managers they are essentially coordinators and influencers, not bosses in the conventional sense. They should also have a high frustration quotient, because things will constantly be going awry despite their best efforts to keep them on track.

We have examined only one organizational source of project failure—the divorce of responsibility and authority. There are many additional organizational sources of problems that we will discuss in Chapters Two, Three, and Four. Explicit recognition of these problems and why they arise should greatly help project managers in doing their jobs. If nothing else, it should make them aware that they are not alone in the problems they face on their projects and that a number of these problems are not of their making, but are organizationally induced. With this knowledge, they can spend less time tilting against organizational windmills, and more time working on things over which they have some influence.

Inability to Identify User Needs and to Specify Requirements Adequately. Too often, what the user needs is not what the user gets. This is illustrated in a popular cartoon found on the bulletin boards of many federal workers in Washington, D.C. It shows six pictures of a tree with all sorts of complex and useless paraphernalia hanging from it. Each picture has a different label, such as "What the planning officer suggested," "What government approved," "What purchasing ordered," and so forth. The final picture is of a tree with a child's tire-swing hanging from a branch, and it is labeled "What was actually required."

A project that produces something that is not used or is grossly underutilized is a failure, *even though a product may have been developed on time and within budget.* Sadly, this is a common occurrence. The final deliverable does not really address the user's needs, or it meets with user resistance, so the user does not employ it. What the user needs (or wants) is not what the user gets.

There are various reasons why this happens. For example, the deliverable may have been generated in a top-down fashion and therefore reflect top management's view of the user's needs, as opposed to the user's actual needs. Or the deliverable may reflect the system designer's opinion of what is best for the user (that is, the "expert" opinion), without regard to user sensibilities. Or problems may stem from the fact that the user does not know what it is that he or she really needs.

Frequently, major problems in this vein arise well before the termination of the project. During a midproject review, the user and the project staff are sometimes at loggerheads because they hold different interpretations of what the project specifications mean. At other times, the project staff find themselves bombarded with user requests to change different features of the product being developed, and this can have devilish consequences on the project schedule and costs. And so on, and so on.

What we face here are problems that arise out of inadequate definition of user needs, poorly written project specifications, and midproject changes in these specifications. Inevitably, such problems contribute to cost and schedule overruns, and if the deliverable is never utilized, what results is total project failure. In its projects, the Department of Defense is almost overwhelmed with such problems. We regularly read stories in our newspapers about the development of costly weapons systems that don't do the job they were intended to do, or about hideous cost overruns and schedule slippages. In reading these stories, we typically attribute the problems to corrupt practices by defense contractors and to general government ineptitude. Most of us are unaware that a major culprit behind the Defense Department's project failures is poor needs recognition and inadequate definition of requirements.

Chapters Five and Six focus heavily on user needs and project requirements, because they are issues that all project managers must deal with and are a major source of project failure. Many failures could be avoided if project managers were more sensitive to needs and requirements. In Chapters Five and Six, a number of simple techniques will be offered for defining and monitoring needs and requirements effectively.

Poor Planning and Control. A poorly planned project will likely run into trouble. Good planning is a necessary—though not sufficient—condition for project success. Similarly, good project controls are important. They allow us to determine whether our plan is being carried out properly, and with this knowledge we can make the necessary adjustments to our project to keep it on track. A project with poor controls is a project that is out of control.

The importance of planning and control to project success is widely recognized. Planning and control topics constitute

the bulk of material written in the project management literature. The tools with which project management is so closely
associated—Gantt charts, PERT/CPM charts, resource loading
charts—are planning and control instruments. There is good
reason for this attention to planning and control. First, planning and control are palpable activities of honest-to-goodness
substance. We plan and control budgets; and, because budgets
are denominated in dollars, we can measure what we want and
what we are actually getting. Likewise, planning and control
of schedules permit us to work with another measurable com-
modity—time. We can measure to ten decimal places, if we
want, the precise time when an activity should commence, and
we can measure with equal precision how far off schedule we
are. Planning and control also focus on human and material
resource allocations, again things that are measurable. Because
planning and control are amenable to measurement, we can
easily develop and use tools to help us in our planning and control efforts.

A second reason for the attention directed at planning and
control is that they are so often carried out inadequately. It is
common to have budget overruns because no one planned for
given contingencies, or schedule overruns because no one was
keeping track of whether tasks were being completed in a timely
fashion.

Of the three principal sources of project failure I have
identified here, planning and control are the easiest to deal with,
because good planning and control practices can be readily conveyed to project managers and staff. Organizations, or individual
project managers, can establish routine planning and control
protocols, which, when implemented, will eliminate some of the
more egregious planning and control oversights. Planning and
control procedures can be computerized, and with the explosive
growth in microcomputer usage, we find a proliferation of inexpensive, commercially available budgeting, scheduling, and
resource allocation software.

Not all planning and control issues have been resolved.
One question that frequently arises is "How much planning
and control should we undertake?" This question underscores

a number of trade-offs associated with planning and control. For example, we can have overplanning and overcontrol that stifle creativity and reasonable project modifications. On the one hand, we may harm our project by excessive planning and control; on the other hand, the project may fail owing to a lack of plans and tracking mechanisms.

Chapters Seven and Eight address frequently encountered planning and control problems and offer techniques for dealing with them.

Lesson 2: Making Things Happen

Several years ago, after I had finished a brief planning and control presentation before a group of corporate project managers, one of the attendees approached me in the parking lot as I was about to get into my car. He told me that he had found my presentation interesting but that unfortunately he had not learned anything new. He already knew about the techniques I described, he said, and in fact he religiously employed them in his projects. He also offered that he was pretty good at circumventing some of the more obvious project management pitfalls. However, despite the fact that he was pushing the right buttons and pulling the right levers, his project performance was lackluster; he feared that he would soon be removed from project management responsibilities if things did not improve. "Why," he asked, "can't I seem to make things happen in my projects?"

I spent only a few minutes with the fellow—just enough time to deduce that he wasn't very articulate, was clumsy in his human interaction, and was excessively didactic. Though he made an effort to ask me my opinion of what his problem was, he was not really interested in hearing my views; he interrupted or contradicted me every time I uttered five words. No doubt he *was* following the book in how he ran his projects. If my experience with him was at all typical of his dealings with people, however, there was no great mystery about why he was not effective in getting things done.

As I mentioned earlier, the effective project manager has

mastered the important lesson of avoiding pitfalls. However, this is not enough. To be truly effective, the project manager must also be able proactively to guide the project forward in the best manner possible—to make things happen.

This is easier said than done. To a large extent, project guidance has something to do with leadership and all that it implies. A large body of literature has been written on leadership, some of it scientific, most of it anecdotal and inspirational. It also has something to do with the concept of entrepreneurship, since the chief trait of an entrepreneur is the ability to make things happen. Just to muddy the waters further, let me add that it also has something to do with politics, where politics is defined as *the ability to influence others*. Since project managers have little direct control over anything, to get things done they must be effective in influencing others to do their bidding; that is, they must be good politicians.

Organization of This Book

This book is divided into three major parts, each corresponding to one of the three major sources of project difficulties described at the outset of this introductory chapter. Chapters Two, Three, and Four deal with organizational factors that contribute to project problems; Chapters Five and Six, with difficulties in identifying user needs and improperly specifying project requirements; and Chapters Seven and Eight, with poor planning and control.

By organizing the book in this way, we focus directly on those issues that are likely to give project managers the most serious headaches. Problems *will* arise in managing projects, so it does not make sense to deal with them obliquely.

How the Realities
of Organizational Life
Affect Projects

Recently I was sitting in a hotel lobby with four experienced project managers and we were idling away the time swapping stories about project management experiences. One manager made a remark that clearly struck a responsive chord in the others. He said, "I spend a lot of time fantasizing about how much I could get done on my projects if one day my company and its budget officers and upper-level managers and purchasing agents and lawyers all went *poof*—evaporated into the stratosphere." His three colleagues vigorously nodded their heads in approval. If this comment were made before an audience of one thousand project managers, I think that you would find most of them nodding their heads in approval also. There is a strong consensus among project managers that projects would be better undertaken outside the usual organizational environments.

It is easy to sympathize with this view. However, there is something about it that is bothersome: it is unrealistic. Projects occur in organizations. To design and manage projects out of their organizational context is similar to designing machinery for a frictionless world. In both cases, we have something that looks good on paper but will not work very well in the real world.

Chapters Two, Three, and Four look at project management from an organizational perspective. They show that to study projects out of the context of their organizational setting is a fruitless undertaking.

In this chapter, we focus on organizational realities and how to work effectively *with* them, as opposed to struggling *against* them. As an introduction to these realities, consider the case of Jerry Wallenstein and his first hands-on encounter with project management and organizational realities. The experiences Jerry faces are common to inexperienced project managers. This case, which follows Jerry from the first to the last day of his project, shows that things can easily get out of hand even when project managers perform competently.

THE EDUCATION OF JERRY. Jerry was delighted when he was made manager of a project to explore the possibility of linking together his company's microcomputers into a local area network (LAN). This LAN could greatly enhance intracompany communications by tying corporate staff together electronically. The number of hard-copy interoffice memorandums floating around the company would be reduced to almost nothing. An electronic bulletin board would alert staff to organization-wide issues. Managers could directly access data stored in the company's central computer. Monthly reports could be conveyed electronically from subordinates to their supervisors. In short, the company could be rapidly propelled into the information age, a possibility that Jerry found to be very exciting.

This project provided Jerry with his first real management experience. He had received his M.B.A. degree directly after finishing college, and then he was hired right out of business school by Globus Enterprises, where he spent two years serving as special assistant to Max Weiner, vice-president of administration. The job gave him plenty of exposure to high-level decision making, but was somewhat frustrating because he was a spectator in the decision-making process, not a performer. Now, with the LAN project, he could do something tangible and have real responsibilities.

Jerry put together a list which he titled "Things to Do." At the very top of the list was the item "Assemble Project Staff." He approached his boss, Mr. Weiner, and asked him how big a staff he would have and who would be on it. "Use anyone you need," Weiner responded. "The important thing is to give me a report on your findings within a month. Your preliminary investigation will give us an idea of how we should go about LANing Globus, and we need that information in time for our next quarterly executive meeting."

Jerry determined that he needed the following people in order to do a good job on his project: a secretary, an assistant, a microcomputer expert, a telecommunications specialist familiar with LAN technology, and a representative from each of the company's five divisions. He reckoned that he, the secretary, and an assistant would be the only full-time workers on the project. Nonetheless, the other members of the project team would have to make a fairly substantial commitment to the project if it was to be completed in a month; each would have to dedicate about 25 percent of his or her time to the project.

According to Jerry's plan, the five divisional representatives would each write a section of the study, detailing the information needs of their divisions and assessing the impact of a LAN system on the productivity of their operations. The microcomputer and LAN experts would work with his assistant to write the technical section of the report. Jerry's chief function would be to coordinate the efforts of the others and to integrate all the pieces into a cohesive whole.

Jerry immediately ran into trouble when he tried to put his team together. His first setback was his inability to get a secretary assigned full-time to the project. Because his division was in the midst of a reorganization, all secretarial staff were already overcommitted. When Jerry went to Weiner with his problem, Weiner nodded sympathetically and told him that, unfortunately, he would just have to make do with whoever was available on a given day.

Jerry's luck in obtaining a full-time assistant was a little better— or so it seemed at first. After spending half a day trying to find someone who was free to work on the project, he came across the name of Bob Roulette, who worked in the Contracts and Procurement Department. Bob, it was reported, was two months from retirement, so his workload was being reduced in preparation for his departure. A one-month job would dovetail nicely with the plans to ease him into retirement.

The easiest team member to recruit was the microcomputer

specialist. Jerry approached the Information Resource Management chief (IRM is located in the Data Processing Division) and told him of his need for a microcomputer and LAN expert. The IRM chief immediately assigned Margaret Block to help Jerry with microcomputer matters. Unfortunately, the company had no LAN experience, so Jerry was told that he would have to go to an outside consultant for LAN expertise.

Jerry met with varying degrees of success in recruiting representatives from the different divisions. He had a good reception from the Finance Division; the vice-president of finance, Kathy Reigstad, announced that it was about time Globus Enterprises entered into the twentieth century and said she would be glad to assign someone from her office to help Jerry on the project. In contrast, his reception at the Data Processing Division could not have been cooler. His request for assistance from the division's vice-president, Sam Ruff, was met with an uncomfortably long and stony silence. Finally, Mr. Ruff said, "I don't fully understand why you and Weiner are initiating something like this. You never even asked us—the experts in these kinds of things—our opinion on the wisdom of setting up a LAN. As it turns out, I've had a couple of our people looking into this issue for several months." He dismissed Jerry without promising cooperation and said something vague about having to "look into things personally."

Jerry was unnerved by his encounter with the Data Processing vice-president. Up until now, all of his experiences at Globus had been quite friendly. He was still brooding about his meeting with Mr. Ruff when he was accosted outside his office by Bob Roulette, his new assistant on the project.

"Listen, Jerry," Roulette said. "As you know, I'll be retiring in just under two months. I'd like to help you on this project of yours, but let me say that I really don't know anything about computers. To tell you the truth, I hate the things. Frankly, I think somebody did both of us a dirty trick putting me on this project. I'll gladly work with you, but don't expect too much from me."

All these things happened by the third day of the project, a Thursday. In order to get the project moving quickly, Jerry tried to arrange a kickoff meeting of all project staff for nine o'clock the following Monday morning. The Data Processing Division still had not assigned a representative, so it would not be represented at the meeting. The Finance Division representative said he thought it was a great idea to get moving so quickly, but unfortunately he would be out of town throughout the week. The other project staff members said that they would attend the meeting, but they sounded less than eager. The only individual who sounded interested in the meeting was Margaret Block, the microcomputer expert. Jerry wasn't sure what he would do about getting a LAN expert. He would talk to Weiner about it next week.

Jerry spent all day Friday, Saturday, and Sunday preparing for the meeting. He put together a five-page preliminary position paper, identified milestones the team members would have to meet, created guidelines for the activities to be undertaken, and read several journal articles on LAN technology. On Monday, at nine o'clock, Jerry arrived at the conference room and found it empty. By nine-thirty, only two other project team members had shown up. Conspicuously absent were his assistant, Bob Roulette, and Margaret Block.

When a much-discouraged Jerry returned to his office, he found a message asking him to call Margaret Block. He called her. She apologized for missing the meeting and explained that her boss in the Information Resource Management Department (part of the Data Processing Division) had told her that he was pulling her off the project. She wasn't sure why.

At one-thirty, Mr. Weiner called Jerry into his office to tell him that he was canceling the LAN project. "All hell's broken loose," he explained. "Ruff went to the big guy and complained that you and I, a couple of amateurs, were running amok, doing things we had no business doing. Sorry, Jerry. You win some and lose some. Next time we'll do better, right?"

"Sure," said Jerry in a daze. He didn't really understand what all this meant. All he could think of was that someone had told the company CEO that he, Jerry, was some kind of amateur. Jerry wondered about his future at Globus.

Organizational Reality:
The Divorce of Responsibility and Authority

Though most of our first experiences with project management are—we hope—not as traumatic as Jerry's, his experiences at Globus illustrate a number of traits common to the great majority of projects. One of the most obvious is that Jerry was given responsibility for getting the job done, but he had very little authority to see to it that his decisions were implemented. This was reflected in his problems in recruiting project team members. It was further evidenced in the fact that he could exercise only marginal control over Bob Roulette, his assistant and the only other full-time team member.

This feature of Jerry's story—the divorce of responsibility and authority—is the rule in project management. Project managers typically have little authority to carry out their work. They have little or no direct control over those people and things that make the difference between project success and failure. Their staff generally are on temporary loan to them. The people who make decisions on whether or not these staff members get promoted, get a pay raise, or get tuition paid for graduate coursework—that is, their true bosses, the people who really count—work elsewhere. Similarly, the material resources they need on their projects—super-minicomputers, mass spectrometers, bulldozers—are usually controlled by others and must be borrowed.

"Well, then," an observer of the project manager's plight might say, "it seems that this problem can be easily addressed. Let's give the project manager authority over all resources—material and human—employed on the project." Easier said than done—and, in most cases, bad management. It is not an accident that project managers have so little direct control over anything. It stems from the very nature of projects, as well as organizational requirements that resources be not squandered but used efficiently. To see this, we need merely reflect on several features of the basic definition of projects that was posited in Chapter One. Consider the following:

- *Projects are temporary.* Projects occur in a finite period of time. Jerry's project, for example, was supposed to last one month. Projects can last minutes, hours, days, weeks, months, or years. Unless they are crucially important major projects, the organization in which they are carried out existed before their beginning and endures after their end. For that reason, it is often difficult on economic grounds to justify the assignment of project staff and material resources to the project on a full-time basis.

- *Projects are unique.* Projects are one-of-a-kind undertakings. At Globus Enterprises, for example, feasibility studies of LAN systems are not a daily occurrence. Projects are structured to address momentary needs.
- *Projects are systems.* Projects are comprised of different pieces linked together in intricate ways. Individuals with specialized skills often work on the individual pieces. On the LAN project, the team was structured in such a way that most of the team members would bring their own specialized skills to the project (for example, knowledge of microcomputers, knowledge of the workings of the Finance Division, typing skills). Often, though, the skills are so specialized that they are employed only briefly. It is not at all uncommon to have the composition of the project team continually changing as the project progresses along the project life cycle. The person who can be usefully employed full-time on a project is the exception rather than the rule.

The very nature of projects requires that human and material resources be borrowed rather than permanently assigned to the undertaking. As long as project managers are dealing with borrowed resources, they have limited control over them. This reality overwhelmed Jerry in the one week that he was "managing" his project. The narrative is full of instances in which he is incapable of getting people to do what he needs to have done. He cannot get a secretary assigned full-time to his project. His full-time assistant makes it clear that he is just treading water until his retirement, and he doesn't even show up for the important project kickoff meeting. Jerry finds a cooperative and competent colleague in Margaret Block, the microcomputer expert; but, owing to the political dynamics of the situation, she is pulled off the project by her boss. Because Globus does not have a LAN expert, Jerry will have to obtain the necessary expertise from an outside consultant, over whom he may or may not be able to exercise some degree of control.

From Jerry's perspective, the problem is that, although he is project manager of the LAN feasibility study, *he is not the boss*. It would be understandable if, after spending hours mulling over his first project debacle, he had concluded that he could have been successful on the project if only Mr. Weiner had made him a boss—someone who could exercise clear and unambiguous authority over the resources he needed to employ in his work. While understandable, this would be a naive conclusion and would suggest that Jerry did not learn much from his unpleasant project experience. To be boss, he would have to possess control over the career development of all the personnel working on the project, and in view of the nature of his small project, this would be impractical.

Nurturing Authority

If project managers lack authority, and this presents a problem for them, why don't they create and nurture it? Successful project managers do exactly that. They emphasize their strengths and use these strengths to build a base of authority.

Authority is the capacity to get people to take us seriously and to do our bidding. In the old days, kings had authority based on their power, which was embodied in their troops. When the powerful king issued a command, the wise citizen listened and obeyed.

A doctor's authority lies in a knowledge of medicine that allows him or her to heal patients. People certainly take their doctor seriously; they generally follow the regime suggested and swallow the pills prescribed without questioning the wisdom of such behavior.

One of the most common authoritarian characters in our everyday lives is the police officer, an individual whose very survival in some communities depends upon the ability to project an image of authority. In fact, when a community is in the throes of lawlessness and rioting, we often ascribe this situation to "a breakdown of authority."

Advertising specialists recognize that an important consequence of authority is that people do the bidding of those who possess it. Thus, we find sober men and women in medical garb—looking every bit like everyone's image of the family physician—hawking all manner of medication on television, from laxatives to suppositories to analgesics. Not long ago, we even had the actor who had portrayed one of television's most popular doctors selling coffee and suggesting that consumption of decaffeinated coffee was a soothing remedy for frayed nerves!

If project managers want people to take them seriously and to do their bidding, it appears obvious that they have to create and nurture a base of authority. In the project management area, there are five kinds of authority that they should focus on. The first three are organizational: formal, purse-string, and bureaucratic. They are rooted in the specific organizational setting in which project managers find themselves. The two remaining kinds of authority, technical and charismatic, are personal. They are intrinsically tied to the project manager's personality and achievements.

First, we will look at the three organizational sources of authority.

Formal Authority. All project managers possess some degree of formal authority to carry out their work. This formal authority is automatically conferred on them as soon as they have been appointed to the project. The appointment itself suggests that the powers that be have confidence that a particular individual can carry out a project, and this further suggests that he or she has backing from above, no matter how tenuous.

If the formal authority project managers possess is no more than a vague sense that someone somewhere has confidence in their abilities, that authority will not be very helpful to them in getting people to do their bidding. If, in contrast, the corporate CEO makes a big show of appointing the project manager and makes it clear to everyone that the new appointee has his or her fullest backing, people in the organization will be more ready to take note of the project manager's wishes. In this instance, the formal authority can be translated into real, operational authority.

Most project managers do not receive the kind of clear-cut upper-management backing that will make whatever formal authority they have very meaningful. Usually, the little formal authority they have is not enough to offset other forces that keep them from exercising direct control over people and material resources.

Preference for and dependence on formal authority is common among inexperienced, insecure, and unimaginative project managers. What they find most appealing about it is that authority is *conferred* upon them; they don't have to work at developing it. Unfortunately for them, the authority they derive in this way is often more apparent than real.

Purse-String Authority. If project managers have some budgetary discretion and use it effectively, they can exercise authority of the purse strings. Clearly, this kind of authority is effective only in dealing with individuals who are affected by a project manager's budgetary actions. For example, it is particularly useful in dealing with outside vendors and contractors, whose livelihood depends on payment for goods and services delivered.

The power of purse-string authority can lie in both the offering of a carrot and the wielding of a stick. Promises of future business, or the payment of an incentive bonus for work done before scheduled delivery, may encourage outside vendors and contractors to do a good job. Threats of withholding payment for poor work may stimulate lackadaisical vendors to improve their performance; however, by the time it becomes obvious that a stick is necessary, poor schedule, cost, or quality performance may have already seriously jeopardized the project.

Bureaucratic Authority. History is filled with examples of individuals who attained power in their organizations through the quiet mastery of bureaucratic skills. The colorless Joseph Stalin is a case in point. In vivid contrast to Lenin's charisma-based authority, Stalin's authority lay in his capacity to manipulate the Communist Party and government bureaucracies to do his bidding. He focused on the smallest details of personnel assignments and was a master of organization charts.

To project managers with good bureaucratic skills, the organization is not an obstacle to the accomplishment of project objectives. In fact, knowledge of the organization and the rules that make it tick is a positive blessing. Bureaucratic managers do not struggle against the organizational current, but rather go with the flow. Their authority is based precisely on an understanding of the importance of filling out the paperwork properly, meeting seemingly arbitrary due dates for project status reports, and knowing the details of the organization's procurement procedures.

Formal, purse-string, and bureaucratic authority are all derived from the specific organizational circumstances in which they arise. We now look at authority that arises not from organizational circumstances but from the personality and achievements of project managers themselves.

Technical Authority. Technical workers typically have a high degree of respect for technical competence. Often they judge the value of other workers according to their technical capabilities. In a laboratory environment, for example, a researcher may hold a fellow scientist in low esteem because he or she "hasn't published anything worth a damn in five years."

The emphasis that technical workers place on technical capabilities often causes them to resent management's authority over them. I have heard many researchers in laboratories complain about working for bosses who "aren't all that sharp technically." One scientist I know quit his job on this account and set up his own company, vowing that he'd never again work for someone who wasn't smarter than he. For an employee who measures a person's worth according to whether or not he or she understands quantum mechanics, working for a boss who never went beyond first-year calculus may be a bitter pill to swallow.

In our society, we tend to have a high regard for people of technical or intellectual accomplishment. Consider the public's adoration of past men and women of great intellectual accomplishment, such as Thomas Edison, Marie Curie, and Albert Einstein. On a more mundane level, we are in awe of the wizards of our own organizations: the people who can program computer code ten times faster than the norm, or who are masters of the intricacies of the tax code, or who have managed to secure two patents a year over the past fifteen years. When these people speak, we listen. If they make a request of us, it is an honor to oblige them.

Project managers who possess technical authority can use this authority to great effect. They can get people to do their bidding, not because they control salaries or prospects for promotion but simply because their staff respect their technical competence.

Lack of technical competence may preclude an individual from managing technical projects. On projects that require the project manager to carry out technical tasks—a common arrangement in, for example, small software development projects—this is understandable. But frequently a technical background is required of project managers even when they do not carry out technical duties. In part the rationale here is that only a technically trained individual can appreciate the technical nature of the problems faced by the project staff. Perhaps more significant is the feeling that nontechnical managers lack credibility with their staff and will not be taken seriously by them. That is, nontechnical managers lack the technical *authority* to manage the project.

Charismatic Authority. Perhaps the most useful kind of authority is charismatic. The project manager who possesses charismatic authority is able to get others to listen to him and do his bidding through the force of his personality. The principal appeal of such authority is that it is ''portable''; it can be carried from project to project and from organization to organization. If properly developed, it can be employed by the project manager to gain some influence over the many actors in the project environment who can make the difference between project success and failure.

Charismatic authority is rooted in a number of different traits that the project manager possesses. The charismatic manager often possesses a sense of mission, has a good sense of humor, is empathetic to staff needs, is enthusiastic, and is self-confident. The charismatic manager is a *leader*.

It should be clear that project managers who do not possess formal or purse-string or bureaucratic or technical or charismatic authority are in trouble. Furthermore, if they possess only one of these forms of authority, they probably are still in trouble. For example, if a project manager has only charismatic authority, staff may enjoy his management style but ultimately may perceive him as all form and no substance. If his bureaucratic skills are not well honed, he may miss crucial deadlines for filling out nuisance forms. And so on.

In general, project managers should develop and nurture at least two forms of authority. Other things being equal, project managers possessing three forms of authority are even better off. The importance of authority is that it gives project managers some leverage over the many other actors in the project environment. Without such leverage, project managers are not really in control of their project.

The Full Project Environment

Jerry's project experience has given us only a small glimpse of the project environment. It is something like looking through a keyhole into a room. With some effort, we are able to discern a chair here and a lamp there, but at best we have only a vague idea of the full layout of the room.

A view of the full project environment reveals a situation that—from a management point of view—is extremely complex. Figure 2.1 portrays the full project environment from an Ptolemaic point of view: the project manager stands at the center of things. Of course, this is a distorted view of the project environment. Project managers must cope with a Copernican reality. Like the earth, they are but a small speck off in a corner of their galaxy.

A survey of this figure confronts us with a couple of interesting facts. First, the sheer number of actors that project managers must deal with assures that they will have a complex job guiding their project through its life cycle; problems with any of these actors can derail the project. For example, suppliers who are late in delivering crucial parts may blow the

Figure 2.1. The Project Manager's Operating Environment.

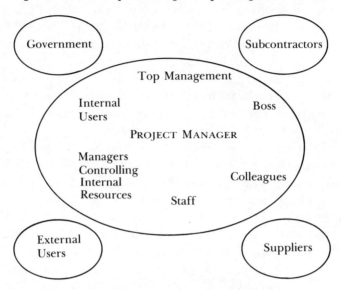

project schedule. To compound the problem, project managers generally have little or no direct control over any of the actors portrayed. The figure also shows that project managers often have to deal with the environment external to the organization, as well as with the internal organizational environment. What we have here is an extremely complex management milieu—certainly more complex than what a manager in a retail store or in a manufacturing environment faces.

In dealing with human relations on projects, books and courses usually focus on project managers' relationships with their staff. These relationships certainly are important and warrant close scrutiny. It should be noted, however, that relations with the other actors included in Figure 2.1 are also important, because, as was noted above, problems with any one of them can derail the project. On a more positive note, it might be added that good relations with any of them can aid project managers tremendously. Let us look in some depth at these actors and their relationships to the project manager.

Top Management. Top management in the organization may or may not be directly involved with a project manager's project. Large projects are highly visible, and it is likely that their project managers will have direct interaction with top management. IBM's project to develop the 360 line of mainframe computers is a well-known example of a project that was watched closely by top management.

Obviously, managing a high-visibility project has both advantages and drawbacks. On the plus side, the highly visible project is more likely to have top-management support, which means that it will be easier to recruit the best staff to carry out the project, as well as to acquire needed material resources. This visibility can also significantly enhance the project manager's professional standing within the organization.

On the minus side, an obvious shortcoming of the highly visible project is that failure will be quite dramatic and visible to all. Furthermore, if the project is a large and expensive one (and highly visible projects usually are), the cost of failure will be more substantial than for a smaller, less visible project. Another negative feature of highly visible projects is that top management may find the temptation to meddle in them irresistible, leading to what project managers call *micromanagement*. Micromanagement by top management puts project managers in an awkward position. It takes strong, self-confident, and brave project managers to resist the intense second-guessing of their efforts by the organization's top brass.

With low-visibility projects, direct top-management involvement is unlikely. However, top management can still have a major impact on how the project is carried out, because it sets the tone for the whole organization. For example, if top management establishes an atmosphere of free and open communication in the organization, project managers and their staff are more likely to be honest in reporting successes and failures. If, on the other hand, top management creates an atmosphere in which failure is not tolerated, it is likely that project managers and their staff will be less than honest in reporting progress (or lack of it).

Boss. The importance of the boss to project managers is obvious, since the boss plays a significant role in creating the daily working environment, and since he or she is also instrumental in determining project managers' career prospects within the organization.

Our boss can make life in the organization reasonably comfortable or make it painful. Typically, the boss decides what our assignment is and who can work with us on our project. If things go wrong on our project (and they probably will), it is nice to have an understanding and supportive boss who will go to bat for us if necessary. If, on the contrary, the boss pounces on us at the first sign of trouble, or disowns us, our lives can be very uncomfortable.

Colleagues. Fellow project managers and other peers working in the project manager's organization can be friends, foes, or—quite commonly—a little bit of both. They can be friends in at least two senses. First, they can be useful resources, providing a project manager with important information or human or material assistance. Second, they can serve as helpful allies in getting things done within the organization. For example, while individual project managers may not have enough clout to get their company to purchase what they perceive to be a necessary piece of equipment, in concert with their colleagues they may possess sufficient collective influence to release funds for the purchase.

Colleagues can also be foes. An obvious source of conflict between colleagues is resource scarcity. It is not uncommon for project managers to find themselves competing against their fellows to get good staff or necessary equipment. If this competition is undertaken in a friendly spirit, it need not get out of hand. Colleagues may also be foes in the sense that, as they climb the organizational hierarchy, competition grows for increasingly scarce positions.

Staff. It has been noted several times that the staff project managers have available to them are usually borrowed rather than assigned to the project on a permanent, full-time basis. Recognizing this fact, project-oriented organizations occasionally organize themselves into a matrix structure. A pure matrix structure is pictured in Figure 2.2. Running along the horizontal axis, we have functional groups that serve as resource repositories. The engineering department is filled with a wide assortment of engineers, the data processing department is peopled with programmers and analysts, the finance department is filled with accountants and financial experts, and so on. On the left side of the matrix, along the vertical axis, we have individual projects that present specific resource needs. Project A, for example, has a need for engineers and data processing personnel. When this need ends, the engineers and data processing workers return to their respective functional groups, where they are available for work on other projects.

Figure 2.2. Matrix Structure.

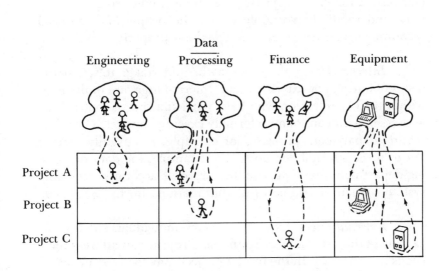

The matrix structure formally incorporates what has been noted several times: because of the temporary, unique, and complex character of projects, it makes more sense to have a project borrow resources on an as-needed basis than to assign resources full-time to the project throughout its duration.

The driving force behind matrix management is efficient employment of resources. While the matrix approach may reduce resource inefficiencies, it still does not resolve the project managers' fundamental problem in dealing with their staff: their workers are only on loan to them and owe allegiance elsewhere—usually to their functional groups and their functional group manager.

Managers Controlling Internal Resources. One special category of colleague that is particularly important to a project manager is other managers who control needed resources. Because project managers are typically in a position of borrowing resources, their relations with the people controlling these resources are especially important. If their relations are good, they may be able consistently to acquire the best staff and the best equipment for their projects. If relations are not so good, they may find themselves unable to get the people and material resources necessary to get the job done properly.

Internal Users. Projects may be undertaken to satisfy the needs of internal or external users. Internal users are individuals within the organization who have particular needs that will be addressed by means of an internally executed project. Data processing department projects, for example, are usually carried out to meet internal demands. For example, the data processing department may upgrade the corporate accounts receivable system or help an office in its automation effort.

External Users. External users are individuals and organizations in the external environment. Projects can address their needs in two ways. In the first, a project may focus on developing a product or process that will eventually be marketed to outside consumers. In this case, there is no guarantee that the consumer will want to buy the product or process, so the project faces the serious risk that it might fail in the marketplace. In carrying out the project, project managers must be conscious of producing something that will succeed in the market. If they are producing an important new product, it may be especially crucial that they complete their project in a timely fashion; if they do not, the product may lose its competitive edge. The business press is filled with stories of companies announcing the forthcoming introduction of a new product and then being embarrassed when the product hits the market several months behind schedule.

Projects also address external user needs through contracts (see Chapter Eight for more details.) The government, for example, commonly funds contractors to carry out desired projects. Here project managers have a clear idea of who the user is; given this knowledge, they are obliged to maintain good communications with the user, to make sure that they are indeed meeting the user's needs. This is easier said than done. As we shall see in Chapters Five and Six, users often do not have a precise idea of what they want. Consequently, user needs tend to change as the project evolves and the user gains a better appreciation of precisely what the project is developing. In such circumstances, project managers must balance their desire to satisfy the user with knowledge that constant changes to the project will lead to time and cost overruns.

Government. Most project managers do not have to deal with government in their projects. However, those working in certain heavily regulated environments—for example, in the pharmaceutical, pesticide, or herbicide industries—must be fully conversant with government regulations that bear on their projects. Not only do they face the problems common to all project managers, but they must work under additional stringent regulatory constraints as well.

Subcontractors. There are times when organizations do not have sufficient skills or capabilities to undertake all project tasks themselves. This is often true of very large, complex projects and of construction projects in general. Under these circumstances, work is farmed out to subcontractors. Project managers working with subcontractors must keep close tabs on the subcontractors' performance, since the success of the project will depend in part on their work. Any number of problems can arise with subcontractors. The quality of their work may be substandard, or they may run into cost overruns, or they may face schedule slippages. Keeping tabs on them is not easy, since they operate outside the project manager's immediate organizational environment. It is hard enough trying to keep tabs on individuals one encounters on a daily basis within one's organization; keeping tabs on outsiders is even more difficult.

In working with subcontractors, the project manager should have substantial knowledge of the provisions in the contract with the subcontractor, as well as a rudimentary knowledge of contract law.

Suppliers. Many projects are heavily dependent upon goods provided by outside suppliers. This is true, for example, of construction projects, where lumber, nails, brick, and mortar come from outside suppliers. If the supplied goods are delivered late or are in short supply or are of poor quality, or if the price at delivery is higher than the quoted price, the project may suffer seriously. Many construction projects are thrown off schedule because required construction materials did not arrive on time, or because the delivered goods were of such poor quality that the delivery had to be rejected.

Reliable suppliers are very important to successful project management. The Japanese have long recognized this in the manufacturing sector. Major Japanese corporations dedicate a good deal of attention to their relationships with suppliers, and the famed *kanban* system, in which supplies arrive at the plant the day they are to be used ("just in time"), has been an important factor in Japan's phenomenal success at producing high-quality goods at a low price.

Project managers have so many balls to juggle that they are often tempted to downplay potential supplier problems in order to focus their attention on other crucial actors in the project environment. "These suppliers are professionals, and I will assume that they will behave in a professional manner," they say to themselves. The project manager who operates on this assumption, and consequently pays little attention to possible supplier problems, may be in for a number of nasty surprises.

The Politics of Projects

Anyone who has operated in a political environment recognizes that politics is the art of influence. The fundamental job of candidates running for public office is to influence a majority of the electorate to vote for them. This is what the speeches, the kissing of babies, and the paid political advertisements are all about. Once in office, the politicians are busy influencing other politicians to back them on legislative proposals, to make them chairpersons of important committees, and to release funds for projects that will enrich their constituencies; the purpose of all this effort is to influence the electorate to vote for them again in the next election. If you think about it, this ability to influence others to do one's bidding is the single most important asset a politician has.

With rare exceptions, politicians are not inherently powerful people. Generally, they do not have large sums of money that they can use as an instrument of power. They do not flex large biceps to intimidate people into doing what they want. They do not possess invaluable knowledge of the secrets of nature that gives them a hold over others. The power they possess is rooted in their ability to influence others. When they lose this ability, they no longer function effectively as politicians. Even the seemingly omnipotent—such as Winston Churchill during World War II—fall quickly when they can no longer exert sufficient influence over their fellows.

Project managers are something like politicians. Typically, they are not inherently powerful, capable of imposing their will directly on their co-workers, subcontractors, and suppliers. Like politicians, if they are to get their way, they have to exercise influence effectively over others. We saw earlier in this chapter that one way to get others to do one's bidding is to create and nurture authority. But politicians need more than the simple possession of authority; they also need to possess a keen understanding of the overall environment in which this authority is to be exercised. They need to be realists.

Block (1983) defines a process that the good project politician follows. It is reduced here to six steps:

- Assess the environment.
- Identify the goals of the principal actors.
- Assess your own capabilities.
- Define the problem.
- Develop solutions.
- Test and refine the solutions.

The first four steps are designed to help the project manager acquire a realistic view of what is happening. Most project managers, when tackling a project, skip over those steps and immediately begin offering solutions to problems. They are not good project politicians.

Because all projects involve politics, and since these politics often have an important bearing on whether projects proceed smoothly or roughly, it is worthwhile to examine these six steps in some detail.

Assess the Environment. The most important elements in the environment are the other actors involved either directly or indirectly with a project. In assessing the environment, the project manager should try to identify all the relevant actors. This is harder to do than it may seem at first blush. Consider, for example, a project to replace all typewriters in an office with word processors. Good project management practice suggests that we should undertake an analysis of the needs of the users of the word processing system. Who are the users? Secretaries, of course, so we focus our attention on them and the satisfaction of their needs. A little reflection might show, however, that other actors whose needs should be addressed include the secretaries' bosses, whose documents will now be handled in entirely new ways; the office director, who is initiating the project in order to have an office filled with machines that hum rather than clunk; the budget office, which must approve funding for the purchase of the word processors; the information resource management office, which must approve all hardware acquisitions to make sure that new hardware is compatible with existing hardware; and the training office, which must determine who should receive training on the word processors. Because each of these actors could derail the project, we would be poor politicians if we did not give consideration to their particular interests in the project.

Once the relevant actors have been identified, we try to determine where the power lies. In the vast cast of characters we confront, who counts most? Whose actions will have the greatest impact?

Identify Goals. After determining who the actors are, we should identify their goals. What is it that drives them? What is each after? In examining their goals, we should not shy away from speculating about psychological motivations, since these may be more powerful than purely work-related motivations.

We should, of course, pay attention to overt goals. However, we should also be aware of the hidden agenda, goals that are not openly articulated. In the word processing example, one overt goal of the office director might be to increase productivity in document production, while a hidden goal might be to have the most modern-looking office in the organization. To satisfy both the overt and hidden goals, the project manager should consider purchasing high-quality word processors that also have a space-age look to them.

In dealing with both overt and hidden goals, we should focus special attention on the goals of the actors who hold the power. By knowing who holds the power, and by recognizing their overt and hidden goals, we reduce the likelihood of making gaffes that upset those people whose actions have great impact. Furthermore, we can use our knowledge in a positive way to determine how we can influence these people to help us achieve our project goals.

Assess Your Own Capabilities. Know thyself. Project managers should have a good idea of their strengths and weaknesses and should be able to determine the bearing of those traits on the project. Self-assessment is a crucial step in developing a realistic outlook on the project and its environment. If project managers have a distorted view of their own capabilities, the project is likely to run into trouble.

Particularly important capabilities are the ability to work well with people and the ability to communicate one's ideas. Project managers who are basically inarticulate should not offer to make weekly progress presentations to higher management, since these presentations will only highlight their poor ability to communicate. If weekly management reviews are necessary, inarticulate managers should rely heavily on articulate staff members.

In assessing their own capabilities, project managers should also be sensitive to their personal values. To a large extent, our value systems define who we are. They are the perceptual filters that determine how we view the world, and they offer us guidance on how to behave. Project managers are not automatons emerging from a common template. Their decisions are governed by their value systems. Some project managers may see their project as one small element in their broader life, whereas others may subordinate everything to the project. Operationally, the first project managers will be less willing to put in overtime on weekends, while the second may eat, sleep, and drink project efforts round the clock. Project managers who are sensitive to their personal values will avoid situations that will generate value conflicts; or, if these conflicts are unavoidable, they will at least understand the sources of the conflicts.

Define the Problem. Only now, after project managers are thoroughly familiar with their project environments and their own capabilities, are they ready to intelligently define the problems facing them. The problem-definition effort should be systematic and analytical. The facts that constitute the problem should be isolated and closely examined. The basic assumptions underlying the approach to defining the problem should be understood. Over and over again, the following question should be raised: "What is the *real* situation?" By taking this approach, project managers are unlikely to naively define the problem according to superficial realities.

Develop Solutions. Too often project staff begin the whole process here. They start offering solutions before they fully understand the problem. Needless to say, with such an approach the solutions they offer are not very useful. However, if they can exercise self-control and refrain from offering premature solutions while they carry out the first four steps discussed here, the ultimate solutions they develop will have the important advantage of being realistic and relevant to the *real* problem that must be addressed. Consequently, they diminish the likelihood of project failure—that is, of producing deliverables that are rejected, underutilized, or misutilized by end-users.

Test and Refine the Solutions. The solutions that staff devise in the previous step will be rough, requiring further refinement. Solutions must be continually tested and refined. If project staff have done the proper spadework with the first five steps, this last step should involve no major rework effort, but rather should focus on putting the finishing touches on intelligently developed, realistic solutions.

There is nothing very novel about these six steps. They incorporate a good commonsense outlook. The most remarkable thing about them is that they are rarely followed, *even after project management staff have acknowledged their importance.* I have conducted about fifty nonscientific experiments on my project management students, to see how they tackle problem solving. I give a group of students a case study that describes a typical project management situation and requires students to offer management advice on how the organization in the case should proceed. Although all these students have already participated in detailed discussions of the six steps that lead to more politically sound projects, *I have never had a group that systematically attempted to identify the full roster of actors affected by the project, or a group that consciously took account of the actors' motivations, or a group that spent any time trying to uncover the hidden agenda implicit in the project situation.* Rather, what the groups typically do is to immediately commence offering solutions to the problem as stated in its most superficial form. It is usually apparent that these early solutions are woefully inadequate, so the groups spend most of their time refining and reworking their original efforts. Generally, the problem they are working on remains superficially articulated, a one-dimensional solution in a three-dimensional world.

After the students have finished with their exercise, I point out to them that they have ignored the fundamental precepts of developing deep, rich, and realistic solutions to problems. I give them a new case study and explicitly ask them to employ the six-step methodology discussed here. The resulting solutions are vastly superior to the earlier solutions. The solutions now take into account a broader array of actors, hidden agenda, and personal values; consequently, they are more viable than their one-dimensional counterparts.

Conclusion

Projects are carried out in organizations, and a thorough understanding of their organizational context is necessary for project success. This obvious point is easy to lose sight of as project managers wrestle with the intricacies of PERT/CPM charts, resource loading charts, and budgets. Too often we confuse the *management* of projects with mastery of the well-known budgeting and scheduling techniques that have been developed as project management tools. The tools are easy to learn. An understanding of organizational intricacies is not. The most effective project managers are those who are as skilled in understanding the organization in which they work as they are proficient in using the basic scheduling and budgeting tools.

Capable People:
The Heart of Every Project

In this chapter, we look at the role of people in projects. First, we focus on a number of broad people issues that are pertinent to projects. Who makes decisions? What do we look for in our project staff? What can we do to cope with chronic shortages of personnel to help us get our projects completed?

In the next section of the chapter, we examine a valuable tool that can help us improve our insights into what makes us, our staff, our boss, our vendors, and our clients tick. This tool is the Myers-Briggs Type Indicator, based on the work of Carl Jung. It helps us avoid putting square pegs in round holes and enables us to understand that conflict is rooted, to a large extent, in differences in the ways that people perceive and judge the world around them.

In the third section of the chapter, we turn our attention to the project manager. We know that project managers are concerned with getting the job done—on time, within budget, and according to specifications. But what other responsibilities do they have? What management styles do they practice, and under what circumstances?

General Issues

Project managers, like people who fish or play the ponies, enjoy telling others the secrets of their effectiveness. One of the most successful project managers that I know, vice-president of operations of a *Fortune* 500 firm, is particularly proud of his ability to pick good people for his projects. "You know, good people are the scarcest resource on a project," he says. "The way I find the best people is to look for the busiest people. During my twenty-five years as a project manager, I always selected for my projects the busiest people I could find. I stayed away from those people who were readily available."

The point this man makes is that the best project staff are heavily in demand. They are kept busy because everyone wants to use them. What is especially interesting is that, although impossible demands are placed on their time, these people figure out ways to get the job done. Sometimes it seems as if the more work you pile on them, the better they do. Available people, on the other hand, make this man nervous. "Why are they so available?" he asks. "Is there a reason why no one is using them?"

People are a project's most important asset. Whether a project succeeds or fails will likely be determined by the caliber of the people working on it. Unfortunately, this is often forgotten by many of us who write project management textbooks and who offer project management seminars. Rather than focus on people, we focus on techniques. We spend most of our time teaching approaches to selecting projects, networking project tasks, and estimating costs. There is a good reason for this preoccupation with technique: it is readily teachable. As an educator, I like teaching techniques, because in a matter of a few hours I can show students how to master PERT/CPM scheduling; what's more, *I can determine through tests whether they have learned their lessons well.* Students conspire with instructors in this little game, because they want tangible benefits from their studies—palpable evidence that their time was well spent.

The focus on technique distorts our view of what happens on projects. For the most part, projects do not fail because people do not know how to employ advanced project scheduling and budgeting techniques. I have never heard of a project failing because a PERT/CPM network crashed. However, I have heard of many projects becoming unglued because top management issued unrealistic directives to project staff, or the skills level of project staff was inappropriate to project needs, or lack of leadership led to aimlessness in project implementation.

It is only recently that organizations have begun putting people on center stage in their operations. This sounds odd in view of the fact that management *theory* has placed people at the heart of the enterprise for three decades, as witnessed in the works of Douglas McGregor, Abraham Maslow, and Frederick Herzberg. For years, thousands of undergraduate and graduate business students have been required to read the works of these and other organizational theorists, so how can I make such an assertion about management *practice*? In part, the assertion is based on my personal experience in dealing with hundreds of managers in many different organizations. What I term *macho management* is alive and well in America. It is still an unsettling experience for me to sit in on management discussions where I hear managers talk about gutting an opponent, cutting a dissident manager off at the knees, and chopping heads if staff don't soon "get their [expletive] together."

There is objective evidence to support my assertion as well. Sales figures show that one of the biggest publishing bonanzas in history was Peters and Waterman's (1982) *In Search of Excellence*, a book that was a top-ten best seller in America for more than a year and that, when later published in paperback, dominated the paperback market for months. This book preaches the simple message that in the most successful companies people count. If you are nice to your staff and give them some degree of meaningful responsibility, they will perform well for you. For the most part, the book is a restatement of organizational behavior material taught in an introductory undergraduate management course. Yet the business press is filled with stories of corporate CEOs buying scores of copies of the work and distributing it to their managers as if this book contained completely new revelations. Other works written in a similar vein also caught on—for example, *The One Minute Manager* (Blanchard and Johnson, 1982) and *Theory Z* (Ouchi, 1981). In the early 1980s, American management finally discovered that organizations are comprised of people and that people make the difference between success and failure!

The traditional management approach is top-down in orientation, looking much like a military command system. Bosses give orders; workers obey. This system reflects a view of human nature that perceives workers as solely concerned with satisfying certain material needs and incapable of taking meaningful initiative. It also reflects the social viewpoint of a highly stratified society—one such as existed in the United States and Europe up to the time of World War II. This view held that some people are born to lead, while the masses are born to follow.

The traditional approach is workable in a highly structured environment—that, for example, of a classic manufacturing operation. Here the worker's effort is guided by detailed instructions. Creativity is actively discouraged, since the production system cannot tolerate deviations from the routine—or so it would seem. In the 1970s, Japan showed the world that, even in routine manufacturing, people count. Quality circles, rotating assignments, the *kanban* system, and lifetime employment practices are some of the people-oriented policies employed by the major Japanese manufacturing firms that propelled Japan into a world leadership position in manufacturing.

While the traditional top-down approach to management may be workable in a routine manufacturing setting—and the Japanese have demonstrated that its effectiveness even here is questionable—it is clearly inappropriate in most project environments. In highly routinized construction projects, where building plans have been worked out to the last detail, a fairly substantial degree of top-down management can be tolerated. If building codes say that studs must be set eighteen inches apart, we do not want our carpenter, in an outburst of creative expression, setting them thirty inches apart. However, for information-age projects that are less predictable, decision making must be distributed throughout the project team. There is too much specialization, complexity, and uncertainty for management to serve as an all-knowing decision maker. With information-based projects, knowledge workers are hired because of their special skills and knowledge; in order to apply their expertise effectively, they must be able to make independent decisions.

Who's in Charge Here?

One of the hard-to-answer questions that arise frequently in projects is "Who's in charge here, anyway?" Decision making in projects is often very diffuse, as is illustrated in the following case.

VIDEOGRAPHICS INC. Videographics Inc. is a small company that produces industrial training videotapes and films. Its marketing department determines that there is a strong demand for fire prevention training videotapes. The head of marketing prepares a two-page document in which she broadly describes the nature of the perceived demand and the potential size of the market. She brings her document before Videographics' executive committee, comprised of the company president, the head of operations, the chief financial officer, and herself. Together they estimate the cost of undertaking the new videotaping venture, compute financial returns, and weigh the contribution of a fire prevention training tape to the company's position in the video training market.

The committee decides to proceed with the venture and authorizes a $30,000 budget to carry out the project. The head of marketing is charged with putting together a project plan within two weeks. Before the project can go full steam ahead, the plan must be approved by the executive committee. A project plan is put together by the marketing department, in conjunction with the production department. It is approved with minor modifications by the executive committee.

Roberta Cohen, who has an excellent track record in producing successful training tapes, is made project manager and given six months in which to complete the project. She is asked to present detailed progress reports to the executive committee at the end of the second, fourth, and sixth months. Cohen puts together a core project team comprised of two script writers and a videotape production specialist. In due course, the script writers produce a script and the production specialist works out the technical details of filming the production. Five actors are hired to play the principal roles written into the script. Meanwhile, the marketing department is putting together promotional material and targeting likely customers.

At the first and second progress report meetings, the executive committee suggests some major changes in the production, and these are adopted. Cohen completes the project according to plan, and one month later an intensive effort is launched to sell the new videotape.

The Videographics case illustrates something that is common to many projects: important decisions are made by many different individuals throughout the project. The decision to explore the possibility of launching a project is in this case made by the marketing department. The decision to launch the project is made collectively by the executive committee. Planning decisions are made jointly by the marketing and production departments. Decisions on coordinating project efforts during the implementation stage are made by Roberta Cohen, the project manager. Detailed decisions on how the script should be formulated and how production should be carried out are made by the script writers and production specialist, respectively. Course correction decisions are made by the executive committee members during the scheduled project review sessions. In answer to the question "Who's in charge?" we are not being frivolous if we answer, "To a certain extent, *everyone*'s in charge."

The dispersion of decision making throughout the project structure can, of course, lead to confusion and conflict. This was graphically illustrated in the tragic explosion of the space shuttle *Challenger* in early 1986. In committee attempts to assign responsibility for the accident, it became apparent that many people inside and outside of the NASA organization made decisions that ultimately contributed to the space shuttle disaster. There was no single culprit. Had the space shuttle project been organized in such a way that decision making was more unified, perhaps the *Challenger* disaster could have been averted. On the other hand, it is not at all clear that a more unified decision-making approach is viable with a project of the complexity of the space shuttle. A more unified decision-making approach would no doubt have given rise to other problems (for example, micromanagement) and probably would have increased overall project costs dramatically. Decision making is distributed throughout projects because projects are too complex to be dealt with in a rigid hierarchical fashion with a clear-cut chain of command.

Once again we see, as we did in the last chapter, that project managers are not bosses in the conventional sense. In part, this condition is a reflection of the organizational realities covered in Chapter Two. Project managers typically do not have staff over whom they have direct control, for example.

In our Videographics example, we see that project managers are not bosses in another sense as well—that is, they are not top-down decision makers, the final arbiters in all important project decisions. Typically, they are excluded from some of the crucial decisions made at the outset of a project that set the tone for how things will be carried out. For example, they may not be involved in project selection or planning decisions. Once the project is under way, they often have to defer to judgments made by others—sometimes because the realities of project politics take decisions out of their hands, often because the novelty and complexity of the project require them to depend heavily on the expertise of their staff.

Figure 3.1. Management by Exception.

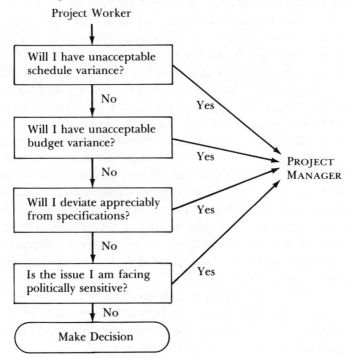

This last point is illustrated in Figure 3.1, which shows that project managers are often practitioners of "management by exception." With this approach, staff are given wide latitude in making decisions, so long as the individual decisions do not have a major unplanned impact upon budget, schedule, and resource utilization, and so long as they do not lead to major political problems. Only when it is obvious that things are going astray does the project manager become directly involved in decision making.

The Perfect Project Staff Member

Let us use our imagination for a moment and conjure up an image of Charles, the perfect project staff member. What is it about Charles that puts him in such heavy demand in his organization?

First, and perhaps most important, Charles is thoroughly committed to the projects he works on. He will do whatever is necessary to get the job done. This means that you can call him while he is attending his little boy's birthday party and he will willingly drop everything to help you out. It also means that he will gladly work eighty-hour weeks, even though he is on salary and is being paid a flat rate for a forty-hour week. What's more, if there is a project emergency and the secretary is out sick, he will type and photocopy his material himself and will personally deliver it by car to the client.

Second, Charles is intelligent and possesses a strong share of common sense. He readily comprehends his assignments and follows instructions carefully. When unanticipated events arise, he is not afraid to deal with them. By the same token, he knows his limitations and does not rush in where angels fear to tread.

Finally, Charles is competent technically. He knows his subject matter well, and when the project manager gives him a task to carry out, she is assured that it will be done efficiently and competently.

In sum, Charles makes his manager's life easier. To the extent that she can count on him to help her out and do a good job, he is freeing her to focus on potential problems that may jeopardize the success of the project.

For many of us, Charles is pure fiction. I know a number of project managers who believe that they are more likely to encounter the tooth fairy than a staff member like Charles. The trait that makes Charles particularly rare is the first one: strong commitment to the project. The scarcity of project commitment has two roots, one organizational and the other psychosocial. We deal first with the organization issue.

Organizational Perspective. The matrix structure found in many organizations discourages strong staff commitment to individual projects. With a matrix system, project staff are drawn out of functional departments and assigned to projects on an as-needed basis. They are temporary visitors who stay with a project long enough to carry out their technical tasks; when these tasks are completed, staff members leave. In addition, they may be applying their expertise to several projects simultaneously, further attenuating their commitment to any given project.

The reward system in a matrix structure does not encourage project staff to put in long hours on projects. Why should they work extra hours for an undertaking in which they have no personal stake? What will their extra effort earn them, other than a pat on the head and a nice letter of thanks written by the project manager and sent to their functional boss?

Under these organizationally rooted circumstances, it is hardly surprising to encounter a reluctance on the part of project staff to commit extra time to projects.

Psychosocial Perspective. I am going to offer a very simple observation here, which for all of its obviousness is surprisingly difficult to drive home: *there is life outside the office.* Many hard-driving managers resist this idea mightily.

Typical project workers are not one-dimensional characters whose lives are completely governed by their jobs. Work is generally only one feature of their life environment. They also have families to contend with, social relations, and a personal set of values that colors their outlook. When they arrive at work, they do not check these nonwork elements at the front door.

Our values strongly affect how we carry out our work. If in our heart of hearts we believe that hard work will invariably pay off, we may be willing to put in eighty-hour weeks for our project. If, in contrast, we hold the view that we only live once and that the world is meant to be experienced and enjoyed, we may cherish our time away from the office, especially our weekends and holidays. If we feel that people should be dealt with forthrightly, we may not have the stomach for the political machinations that projects often involve us in.

The point here is a very simple one that is often overlooked: people working on projects are multidimensional. If project managers do not take this into account, if they treat people as if their jobs were the only thing that mattered, they face two consequences: first, they will be continually disappointed in their staff, because their staff will not live up to their unrealistic expectations; second, they may find that the only people who truly fit into their setting are one-dimensional people. Good people are hard to find. Why narrow our choice only to those prospects who are one-dimensional?

Working Smart, Not Hard

For better or for worse, project managers are not going to encounter very many perfect staff members like Charles. They live in an imperfect world and, rather than rue its imperfections, can better spend their time trying to determine how to use the imperfect resources they have as effectively as possible.

Most project managers focus their efforts on identifying ways to get their staff to work harder. They rack their brains devising carrots to motivate their staff and sticks to prod them on. If they could, they would determine the effectiveness of staff efforts by measuring the number of calories expended by staff on the job. The more calories burned, the better, because calories burned mean hard work.

Such efforts are largely misdirected. For one thing, if project staff do not have a strong commitment to a project, carrots and sticks will not be very effective in getting them to work harder. For another, staff typically are not fully productive on projects, so the issue is not how to get workers to work harder— that is, to prolong the time during which they are ineffectively applying themselves to tasks—but, rather, how to get them to work smarter.

Our efforts should be directed at increasing the productivity of the resources we have. There are several rules that should be followed to help us work smarter.

Do Things Right the First Time. Project managers should do everything they can to make sure that staff members do things right the first time. Studies of manufacturing operations show that reworking defective parts is far more expensive than producing them correctly in the first place. This also holds true in project work. If it takes staff two or three tries before they carry out their tasks properly, enormous amounts of project energy are being wasted. The solution is not to extend the workers' work week by forty hours but to identify ways to get people to do things correctly the first time around.

For example, you may find that your staff are not following your directions properly; this often leads to rework. The problem here is likely rooted in miscommunication. For whatever reason, your staff do not fully understand what is expected of them; so they produce results that have only marginal bearing on the true project requirements. As project manager, you can take steps to reduce such miscommunication. You can explain project requirements carefully to the staff, give them time to reflect upon these requirements (two or three days), and then, when they think they understand them, have them repeat their understanding of the requirements to you. You will probably be surprised at the discrepancy between what *you* thought you communicated to them and what *they* thought you communicated to them. The problem of miscommunication is so prevalent in projects that throughout this book I offer several different strategies for dealing with it. (See especially Chapters Five and Six.)

Set Realistic Goals. If your project is based on a set of unrealistic expectations, you are guaranteed to have insufficient resources to get the job done according to plan. This means that you will be pressured to get staff to put in extra hours on the job. Yet, as we have just seen, if—for organizational or psychosocial reasons—staff have a low commitment to the project, they will be reluctant to work late at night and into the weekend for you. Furthermore, to the degree that they realize that the need for overtime work is a consequence of bad planning, they will resent your requests for help.

The solution to this problem is simple—at least in theory. Plan realistically. Set realistic goals for project staff. Don't put yourself into the position of depending on people you don't have—that is, perfect project staff members who will do whatever is necessary to get the job done. With realistic planning and goal setting, there is less need to have staff work overtime. Consequently, there is less need to have superdedicated workers on your project.

The chief drawback to this solution is that project managers often have little input into the planning process. Plans are often drawn up before a project manager is assigned to the project. When the project manager finds that the plan is woefully optimistic, he or she might try to renegotiate the plan to make it more realistic. Should this approach fail, the project manager can expect to face pressures to get staff to put in overtime hours on the project.

Get Technically Competent People. There are dramatic variations in people's abilities to carry out different kinds of tasks. We have all encountered writers who can write two or three times more polished text than the norm. In software projects, a superprogrammer may be able to generate ten times as much good code in an hour as the average programmer. The obvious lesson here is to employ highly competent people on projects.

I recall clearly the most trouble-free year I had as a manager of a portfolio of several projects. In that year, I was blessed with several staff members who were exceptionally competent technically. My project plans were based on the assumption that I would have average workers helping me. What a delight to find that many of the scheduled tasks were being completed in half the planned time. Because the staff had time to spare, they were able to help out less fortunate project managers in other parts of the organization. No one worked overtime that year, and the quality of our output was the best ever.

Often productivity on tasks is low not because we lack supermen and -women but because the workers carrying out the tasks are not technically competent to do so. For example, I regularly come across office automation projects on which not one single project staff member has received training on information systems. Typically, one or two staff members rush around grabbing any literature they encounter that discusses office technology. They are amateurs and, in spite of their efforts, obviously do not know what they are doing. In the end, they spend great amounts of time miseducating themselves on office automation issues and then blindly make important decisions based on highly imperfect knowledge. What they do poorly over a long period of time could have been done far better by an expert in a fraction of the time.

"We're doing the best we can with what we've got" is a common comment. "We don't have any technically competent experts on our staff." In such a case, it is usually worth the price to hire an outside consultant. The cost of a competent consultant is generally far less than the price paid for poor work produced by highly paid amateurs.

Psychological Types

Over the years, psychologists and management specialists have developed a whole array of tests designed to help us better understand why people behave the way they do. The popularity of these tests is based on the insights they give managers on the roots of conflict, human motivation, and human productivity. They are used for many different purposes—for example, hiring new workers, assigning people to job slots compatible with their personalities, determining special competencies, weeding out workers with obsolete skills, and helping people gain greater self-awareness. One such test, the Thomas-Kilmann Conflict Mode Instrument, measures how much people display competing, collaborating, compromising, avoiding, and accommodating behavior in conflict situations. The T-P (Task-People) Leadership Questionnaire examines the extent to which individuals focus on tasks versus people in work situations. The FIRO-B Awareness Scale examines people along three dimensions: inclusion ("Do you desire strongly to be included in group activities? Do you like to include others?"), control ("Do you prefer being in situations that are well under control? Do you feel a strong need to take control of situations?"), and affection ("Is it important to you to be liked? Do you express affection towards others?").

These tests are not a panacea for resolving organizational difficulties. In fact, there is always a danger that they will be misused. However, when the tests are employed properly, the useful insights they offer managers can be substantial.

The most useful test for project managers is the Myers-Briggs Type Indicator. What is appealing about the Myers-Briggs approach is that it is grounded in solid Jungian theory, has been subjected to extensive empirical testing, is easy to understand, and lends itself nicely to project situations.

Background

People do not behave in uniform ways. They do not possess uniform aspirations. They react differently to different stimuli. In short, people are behaviorally unique. Despite their uniqueness, we find that we can make rough generalizations about them, and from these generalizations we can better understand what motivates them and makes them tick. Some people are aggressive, some are passive. Some work well with others, some don't. Some are curious, some aren't.

Carl Jung, the famous Swiss psychoanalyst, was interested in categorizing people into what he called *psychological types*. In 1923 he published a work describing those types. His work dovetails nicely with research later performed by Katharine C. Briggs, who took Jung's theory and melded it with her ideas. Ultimately, Briggs's effort was further refined by her daughter, Isabel Briggs Myers. The final result is the Myers-Briggs Type Indicator, which is operationalized in a number of psychological tests designed to determine one's psychological type.

The Myers-Briggs approach categorizes people according to where they lie on four scales, each scale reflecting a different dimension of human behavior. They are called the extravert-introvert, sensing-intuitive, thinking-feeling, and judging-perceiving scales. These four scales give rise to a total of sixteen possible psychological pigeonholes that people can be placed into. For example, you might be an extraverted, intuitive, thinking, perceiving type (characteristic of innovators); an introverted, sensing, thinking, judging type (characteristic of administrators); and so on.

Each psychological type has a number of well-documented behavioral traits associated with it. If we know an individual's type, we can quickly develop a good idea of how he or she will behave in different circumstances. Such information can be very useful for project managers, who typically deal with many different people in different kinds of circumstances and who can use guidelines on understanding what makes these people tick.

I will briefly outline the rudiments of the Myers-Briggs approach. However, I will skip over the theoretical basis of this approach. The theory—incorporating the views of Jung, Briggs, and Myers—is rich, interesting, and worth investigating.

The Extravert-Introvert Dimension. An extravert, in the Myers-Briggs schema, is someone who is oriented toward the outer world of people and things, whereas an introvert is oriented more toward the inner world of concepts and ideas. Because they are attuned to what is going on around them, extraverts tend to be practical. They also like to deal with several things at once—to walk and chew gum at the same time, as it were. Introverts, being inner-directed, mull over ideas and live mostly inside their skulls. They tend to be deeper thinkers than extraverts.

So far so good. However, things don't really get interesting from a managerial point of view until you put an extravert and an introvert together in close quarters. Here is what might happen: The extravert has problems coping with the introvert, whom he perceives to be slow, impractical, and positively Teutonic in his dealings with the world. He is particularly irked by the introvert's insistence on tackling only one problem at a time and then pursuing a solution to the problem over a seeming eternity. The introvert, he concludes, is a Johnny-one-note.

He doesn't seem to be very bright, either. The introvert also has problems coping with the extravert, whom he perceives to be incredibly superficial—a jack of all trades and master of none, an individual with no depth. The extravert's instant analyses of problems and his insistence on jumping from topic to topic are especially irritating. Overall, he doesn't seem to be very bright to the introvert.

This scenario shows that two competent individuals of equal intelligence can develop unflattering opinions of each other's abilities *simply because of differences in their orientations to the world.* This circumstance has practical implications for project managers. Consider, for example, the extraverted project manager in charge of running a state-of-the-art software development project. Her technical staff are likely to be introverts who, because of their introversion, are not fully sympathetic with or responsive to external realities such as task deadline dates. She should recognize that the staff's cavalier attitude toward deadlines is a consequence of their introversion rather than a conscious effort on their part to make her life difficult or an indication that they are disorganized. She should also recognize that, from the staff's viewpoint, her extraversion may make her appear overly concerned with what they see to be the superficial aspects of the project, such as deadline dates, and insufficiently interested in the content of the project. Armed with these insights, she can deal with her staff more intelligently than if she based her actions on her gut response to their seeming intransigence.

The Sensing-Intuition Dimension. Jung pointed out that there are two basic ways in which people perceive the world around them. Sensing individuals make full use of their five senses. Their perceptions of the world are based directly on information garnered from sight, sound, touch, taste, and smell. Operationally, they have a high regard for facts—that is, data gathered directly through the senses. Like Sergeant Friday in a popular police drama of the 1950s and 1960s, they are principally interested in "the facts, ma'am, just the facts." They also derive great pleasure from using their senses. Intuitive individuals take information they gather through their senses and "massage" it. They are not concerned with facts for the sake of facts, but rather with the possibilities that the facts suggest. Using their imagination, they are more interested in how things *might* be than with how they actually are. Imaginative people are often strongly intuitive.

As with extraverts and introverts, conflicts can arise between sensing and intuitive types. Sensing individuals tend to see intuitive individuals as playing fast and loose with the facts, while intuitive individuals see sensing types as prosaic and unimaginative.

The Thinking-Feeling Dimension. After people perceive reality (by sensing or intuition), according to Jung, they make *judgments* about its meaning. Some people do this through a cool, detached, logical process. They are thinking types. Operationally, they are more comfortable dealing with things and concepts than with people. Pointy-eared Mr. Spock on the television series "Star Trek" was a pure thinking type. Others base their judgments on more subjective considerations, responses from the heart and gut. Operationally, they are more comfortable dealing with people than with things. They are feeling types.

To illustrate the different judging styles associated with these two approaches, a colleague of mine who is a Myers-Briggs aficionado relates the following tale. When they were first married, he and his wife spent a great deal of time house hunting. He recalls visiting one house in particular. Upon entering the house, he did his usual rounds—checking out the plumbing and wiring, inspecting the gutters and shingles, looking for signs of termites, and so on. After ten minutes, he decided that the house would require a large amount of fix-up work and for this reason would not be worth buying. Having reached this conclusion, he looked for his wife to give her his opinion. He searched several rooms and finally located her in the living room, where she was seated cross-legged in the middle of the floor. She hadn't made it beyond the living room! "This is it, honey," she said. "This is the house. I can feel it in my bones."

This story illustrates an additional interesting feature of the thinking-feeling dimension: there are sex-related differences in our preference for one approach over the other. Some 60 percent of males are thinking types, while some 60 percent of females are feeling types. It is interesting to speculate on how deeply the battle of the sexes is rooted in the fundamentally different processes men and women employ in drawing conclusions about the world around them.

The Judging-Perceiving Dimension. The fourth dimension in the Myers-Briggs schema examines the degree to which people feel compelled to draw conclusions about the world around them. Some people are quick to make judgments; they hold opinions on any and all matters. The idea of loose ends makes them nervous. They would rather make a decision instantly than defer it. Operationally, they are comfortable with order and planning. On the negative side, they may be rigid and closed-minded, and they run the risk of making premature judgments. These are judging people.

Others would rather defer making judgments until there is more information available. They are flexible and open-minded. Unfortunately, they run the risk of being disorganized and falling into the pitfall of procrastination as they await more and more information before making a decision. These are perceiving people.

The conflicts that can arise between judging and perceiving types are obvious. In fact, Neil Simon's play *The Odd Couple* focused on just this difference in outlook between two roommates, one fastidious and organized, the other free-wheeling and disorganized. This play is a veritable case study of the problems that can arise when an extreme judging type and an extreme perceiving type have to deal closely with each other.

Applying Psychological Type Theory to Projects

People who take a Myers-Briggs test are often amazed by its accuracy in describing their psychological characteristics. After receiving the results of his test, one man told me, ''It's uncanny how it describes me. It knows me better than my own mother does. I wonder how it does it?''

There is no magic here. In taking the test, you are asked a number of questions that identify your preferences. For example, one question asks whether as a teacher you would prefer to teach factual information or theory. If you answer factual information, this suggests a preference for sensing over intuition. By answering a whole series of questions, you reveal your overall preferences on each of the four dimensions described above. Taken together, this information puts you into one of sixteen categories. People who fall into a given category tend to share a large number of common psychological traits. Thus, if I know your Myers-Briggs type, I can accurately describe some crucial aspects of your personality, even without knowing you personally.

Knowledge of the Myers-Briggs approach can help project managers deal more effectively with people. There are a number of areas in which the Myers-Briggs approach can do this: in selecting staff, in diagnosing the roots of conflict, in improving relations with staff, and in helping managers know themselves better.

Selecting Staff. The most obvious—and perhaps least useful—application of Myers-Briggs theory is in staff selection. Here management may require all prospective staff members to take a Myers-Briggs test. Routine engineering projects are then staffed with ESTJs (extraverted, sensing, thinking, judging types); design teams are comprised of E- or INTJs (extraverted or introverted, intuitive, thinking, judging types); project marketers are made up of ESFJs (extraverted, sensing, feeling, judging types); and so forth.

Among the problems with using the Myers-Briggs approach in this way, two stand out especially. The Myers-Briggs test does not measure intelligence or technical competence. It may give a manager insight into whether or not an individual will "fit" psychologically in a particular environment, but it will not tell whether this individual is sufficiently knowledgeable to carry out his or her required assignment. In addition, it is usually not practical to rely heavily on the Myers-Briggs Type Indicator for staffing in a project environment, where many factors—including personnel availability and politics—go into staffing decisions.

Diagnosing the Roots of Conflict. Knowledge of the Myers-Briggs approach can be very useful to project managers in diagnosing the roots of conflict in projects. Conflict can arise in many different ways and among many different combinations of actors in the project environment—for example, between project managers and their staff, between project managers and their bosses, and between staff and clients. To the extent that this conflict is based on psychological factors, the Myers-Briggs approach—as the following case illustrates—can suggest tactics for managing the conflict effectively.

SOFTWARE HANDLERS INC. Software Handlers Inc. (a fictitious name for a real company) employs about seventy-five programmers and systems analysts and designs and develops software to meet client needs. A few years ago, Software Handlers struggled with a nagging problem. As with most software developers, a large problem Software Handlers faced was ineffective staff interaction with clients. Staff felt that clients were often naive about computer capabilities, that they didn't know what they wanted, and that they changed their minds frequently. By the same token, Software Handlers' management was receiving an alarming number of complaints from clients about the technical tunnel vision of its staff, their abruptness in dealing with clients, and their inability to do anything that lay beyond their limited ken.

Management instituted a number of policies to deal with this situation, one of which was requiring staff to undergo training on the Myers-Briggs approach. All staff members took the Myers-Briggs test and had the results explained to them by a Myers-Briggs specialist. They were instructed that in dealing with a client they should make a mental assessment of the client's psychological type. Armed with this information, they would, in conjunction with an in-house Myers-Briggs specialist, map out an approach for dealing with the client. For example, if the client were a highly technical type of person (for

*example, an INTP scientist), his or her principal contact in the com-
pany would be a staff member of a similar type (for example, an
INTP or INTJ). On the other hand, if the client were a nontechnical
ESFJ (for example, a manager in a social services agency), it would
be advisable to avoid having an INTP or INTJ type working with
him or her. Instead, he or she would probably get along best with
a staff member of a type similar to his or her own. The management of Software Handlers claims that this approach has substantially decreased staff-client conflict.*

Improving Relations with Staff. The responsibilities of project
managers are different from the responsibilities of project staff.
Typically, what the project manager does is to oversee, coordinate, control, and troubleshoot. Project staff, in general, have
far more focused responsibilities. Their perspective is narrower
than that of the project manager. This means that the basic traits
that make a good project manager may be substantially different
from the traits that make good project staff. In Myers-Briggs
terms, we say that a project manager's psychological type is likely
to be different from that of his or her staff.

     In general, we want project managers to be people who
are practical and aware of their environment. We want them
to have a high regard for factual detail and to be logical and
rational. Finally, we want them to be orderly and capable of
making decisions. What we have describd here, in general terms,
are ESTJ individuals.

     Yet what of managers who are in charge of basic research
projects, where it is probable that a large fraction of their staff
will be ENTP, INTP, and INTJ? It is likely that conflicts will
arise between them and their staff on the basis of differences in
psychological types. ESTJ project managers who are unaware
of the differences in psychological type are likely to be exasper-
ated by their workers, whom they may perceive to be dreamy,
impractical, disorganized, and always speculating about what
might be rather than *what is.* If these project managers try to fit
their staff into an ESTJ mold, chances are that the staff will champ
at the bit and resist. From the staff point of view, management
is trying to impose its superficial and arbitrary sense of "order."

If ESTJ project managers are sensitive to differences in psychological type, they will use their knowledge to enhance the output of their staff rather than try to turn their workers into something they are not. For example, they may encourage staff to publish their research findings and to attend professional conferences, where they can meet other scientifically creative people with similar interests. If project work is humdrum and not challenging, managers may allow staff to spend a certain amount of their time pursuing highly speculative and creative efforts. With such policies, staff are likely to see their project managers as being sensitive to their needs; consequently, they will be more willing to tolerate what they perceive to be superficial and arbitrary project requirements.

Self-Knowledge. As we saw in Chapter Two, for project managers to be good politicians, it is vital that they know their capabilities—their strengths and weaknesses. The Myers-Briggs approach can help them in this effort. It forces them to realize that they cannot be all things to all people. If managers are very practical extravert types, they will probably be a bit weak in doing the things introverts do well—for example, working on a single problem over a long period of time. If they are superlative in dealing with facts (that is, if they are sensing types), perhaps they will be uncomfortable in the realm of speculation, where intuitive types are at home.

Knowing that they cannot be all things to all people, successful managers have the wisdom to surround themselves with staff who can cover their weak points. For example, the project manager who is a bit disorganized and has trouble coming to decisions (a perceiving type) would do well to have a highly organized assistant and advisers who are judging types.

The Project Manager

In this section, we direct attention to project managers. We examine responsibilities they may be assigned, management styles they may adopt, and games they may be forced to play.

Project Manager Responsibilities

As mentioned in Chapter One, if project managers are asked what their responsibilities are, they are likely to respond, "To get the job done—on time, within budget, and according to specifications." Of course, project managers' responsibilities go beyond this. They are also responsible for developing staff, serving as intermediary between upper management and the project staff, and conveying lessons learned to the organization.

Developing Staff. As was mentioned earlier, project management is the accidental profession. People stumble into projects. Rarely do they receive formal training on basic management principles. Project management know-how is conveyed informally; managers learn to carry out projects by working on them and learning the ropes from experienced project managers.

In order to get things done on projects, project managers teach their people the tricks of the trade. This may be done occasionally out of a sense of altruism, but more commonly it is done out of necessity. If you want people to do things right so that you can carry out your project on time, within budget, and according to specifications, you have to show them how best to undertake their tasks. In doing so, you are making them more valuable members of the organization. Whether you realize it or not, you are developing staff. One day, these staff members may assume major project responsibilities and, in their turn, convey project wisdom to their own project staff.

Serving as Management/Staff Intermediary. Project managers are like a slice of bologna in a sandwich. They are situated between higher levels of management above them and the troops below. They occupy a delicate position. On the one hand, they are a part of management and are expected to behave accordingly. They are a conduit for upper-management information directed at the workers. Through them, project staff have a glimpse of organizational goals and upper management's desires. Unfortunately, project managers run the risk of being identified by project staff as flunkies or errand runners for upper management. On the other hand, project managers are part of the troops and provide upper management with a glimpse of the needs, capabilities, and desires of the organization's workers. In this capacity, they must be careful not to be seen as "going native" in the eyes of upper management.

Conveying Lessons Learned. Project managers are great storehouses of practical project knowledge. They gain this knowledge through firsthand experiences with projects, initially as project staff and then as managers. Project successes and failures are burned indelibly in their memory. They can serve their organizations well by effectively conveying lessons learned to their fellow project managers, upper management, and project staff.

Project managers convey their lessons in many different ways, most of which are informal. We have already seen that they pass their knowledge on to new staff. They also convey lessons to upper levels of management by various means. During the selection phase, for example, they may provide advice on whether a given project should be supported, and they may serve as useful members of project evaluation teams. Project managers also convey lessons to their fellow project managers when they are asked advice or during informal sessions in which they exchange war stories.

Management Style

When we talk of management style, we are concerned with the way managers interact with their staff. I focus here on the three basic styles that are frequently discussed in the management literature: autocratic, laissez-faire, and democratic.

Typically, autocratic management is associated with the traditional image of Boss with a capital B. In this management style, Bosses make all the decisions. They exercise tight control over their staff and march around the office with grim expressions. You don't cross Bosses. If Genghis Khan were alive today and working in a modern enterprise, he would be an autocratic manager.

Laissez-faire management lies at the other extreme. With laissez-faire management, anything goes. Staff can do whatever they want. It might even be argued that laissez-faire management is *non*management: *nobody's* in charge.

Democratic management is participative. Managers and staff make decisions jointly. I call it red-white-and-blue management, because it heavily incorporates some of the most cherished American cultural beliefs—everyone is equal, we should all have a say in decisions that affect us, and so forth.

To understand the dynamics of these three styles, and to appreciate their differences, it is helpful to analyze each of them with regard to information flows:

Autocratic Managers. Autocratic managers are not interested in processing information coming from outside themselves. They are not interested in feedback from staff, for example. Note, however, that autocracy has little to do with congeniality. The traditional view is that autocrats are people who are gruff and nasty in their dealings with their staff. This is not necessarily so. Skilled autocrats can be people with a ready laugh and a great sense of humor. They can project an image of openness that leads their staff and colleagues to see them as democratic. They can have an open-door policy, encouraging staff to come in and air their views. However, to the extent that they call the shots and do nothing with the information they receive from their staff, they are autocrats.

An autocratic management style has its pluses and minuses in a project management context. On the plus side, the autocratic approach may be appropriate for routine, low-risk projects, where the staff merely carries out the plan exactly as specified. In such a situation, feedback from staff is not as crucial as in a high-risk, high-flux project. The autocratic approach is also effective when quick decisions need to be made. Since autocrats are not concerned with achieving consensus and gathering large amounts of data on which to base their decisions, they are able to make decisions speedily.

On the minus side, the autocratic approach may lead to demoralization of the staff, since they contribute no meaningful input into the decision-making process. Creative and intelligent knowledge workers want their views to count; if they determine that their bosses don't want to hear their views, they will be unhappy. Another drawback of the autocratic approach is that it may lead to bad decision making, since the boss often bases his or her decisions on insufficient outside information.

Laissez-Faire Managers. In contrast to the highly central-ized decision making of autocratic management, decision making in a laissez-faire environment is very diffuse. (The term *laissez faire* itself is a French term meaning "let do.") We generally find little or no flow of information; or else we may find many flows that are scattered every which way and are not effectively channeled. In a laissez-faire system, project staff may be able to direct feedback to their managers—but, unfortunately, the managers do not act meaningfully on this feedback. As a con-sequence, we find that at their heart the diametrically opposed autocratic and laissez-faire approaches hold one very important feature in common: in both cases, little or no meaningful infor-mation flows from project staff to project managers.

The laissez-faire approach may be effective in state-of-the-art projects on which project managers want to encourage creativity and are reluctant to impose their views on staff. Such freedom of action is likely to bolster morale among highly creative workers who do not like to work under close supervision.

On the minus side, the laissez-faire approach may lead to a ship-without-rudder syndrome. At first, project staff may be delighted to be able to do what they want, but before long the sense of freedom metamorphoses into a feeling of aimlessness. Another important minus associated with laissez-faire manage-ment is that it may be disastrous in situations where quick deci-sions are necessary.

Democratic Managers. Managers with the democratic ap-proach actively seek input from staff before making decisions. Overall, this is probably the most effective management style to employ with American knowledge workers, since it dovetails nicely with the American democratic culture. It should be noted that this approach cannot be employed very effectively in certain other cultural environments, however. Soviet workers, for example, are not likely to know how to respond to a democratic approach, since it is alien to their culture. This can be seen in the complaint of many Soviet émigrés now living in the United States: one of the biggest problems our country faces, they say, is lack of authority and structure!

There are various pluses associated with the democratic approach. First, as we have just mentioned, it fits nicely with American cultural notions. Second, it can lead to better decision making, since it reflects a broad spectrum of viewpoints. Third, it increases the commitment of staff to carry out decisions, because the staff themselves have had a role to play in the decision making process.

The democratic approach also has its drawbacks. One is something that political scientists call the *tyranny of the majority*. This results when a given majority in a democratic system always gets its way, much to the chagrin of what becomes a perpetual minority. An analog in a project management scenario occurs when a given clique always calls the shots. It will not take long for individuals outside of the clique to become discouraged by and disillusioned with how decisions are made on the project. A second drawback of the democratic approach becomes evident when the wrong ''voters'' are polled on their views and decisions are consequently based on incorrect information. For example, a democratic manager may make a great show of getting feedback from his staff before making some important decisions, but if the staff he consults are not technically competent to offer meaningful advice (that is, if he has polled the wrong voters), his decisions will not be based on valid information. A third drawback of the democratic approach is that it may be ineffective when quick decisions are needed.

Choosing a Management Style

In actual project situations, it is neither possible nor advisable for project managers to pursue one style 100 percent of the time. Effective project managers find that their management style reflects the circumstances facing them. A project manager may adopt a laissez-faire manner with her closest staff during the creative design phase of a project and then adopt a democratic approach during the more routine implementation phase. She may determine that the only way she can get good results out of a troublesome supplier is by behaving in an autocratic fashion with him, yet she may take a laissez-faire approach with another supplier who has proved to be very reliable over the years.

The style employed by project managers can have a dramatic impact on the outcome of their projects. Let me give you an example. The worst-run construction project I have ever come across was headed by a new construction superintendent who came out of his company's sales department; he had been given project responsibilities as a reward for good sales performance. Because this individual was unfamiliar with the nuts and bolts of construction, he deferred all project decisions to his subcontractors—that is, he adopted a 100 percent laissez-faire approach. Anyone familiar with the building industry recognizes that one major role played by the construction superintendent is that of autocrat. The superintendent often has to crack the whip with subcontractors, whose own agenda may not correspond to the needs of the superintendent's project. On the project in question, progress ground to a halt as subcontractors did whatever they felt like doing.

The trick is to know which style to apply in different circumstances. This decision depends largely on the good sense of the project manager and his or her capacity to size up situations accurately. It also depends on personality factors—what style or styles is the project manager most comfortable with? It may be that he or she is constitutionally incapable of adopting a democratic or autocratic or laissez-faire style.

Playing Games

I once spent several days visiting an engineering firm that produces telecommunications hardware and software. On the first day, I had lunch with the president and two other executives, and we discussed the president's approach to project management in his organization. His approach was a standard one—perhaps more enlightened than the average, since he was actively concerned with project management issues. However, something he said disturbed me: "One thing I've learned after working with engineers for thirty years is that when you ask them to estimate how long it will take to do something, they always hem and haw and give you a figure that's 20 percent larger than it should be. So whenever one of my engineers tells me it will take so much time to complete something, I lop 20 percent off the figure and tell him to do it more quickly."

Over the next two days, I had an opportunity to talk to a large number of the company's project managers about their work. Most expressed general satisfaction with the work environment, but one critical comment surfaced a number of times: "We're always under tremendous schedule pressure. We're asked to make good estimates about how long it will take to carry out our tasks, but when we submit our estimates, we're always told to perform our work much faster than we say we can. As a result, we spend an awful lot of time working after hours and on weekends so that our schedules don't slip." One project manager confessed to me that he deliberately exaggerated his estimates of task duration, so that when upper management cut it back, the resulting figure would be reasonable.

A month later, I visited a U.S. government research laboratory, where I presented a project management seminar to middle managers. In the morning of the second day of my visit, we were reviewing three charts, showing three projects in various states of disarray in their schedules and budgets. Toward the end of the discussion, I pulled out a fourth chart, which showed a project perfectly on budget and ahead of schedule. It was labeled "Fantasy World," and I told the group that it pictured something that rarely happened in projects. Several of the project managers present burst out laughing. They told me that virtually all their projects looked like the one pictured in the Fantasy World chart. These project managers had learned to manipulate to their advantage the arbitrary fiscal-year requirements of their agency's budget system. Furthermore, each project was structured so that it would consume only 80 percent or so of its budget. A large margin of error was thus built into budget and schedule estimates. When money was left over on a project (and it often was), staff would undertake unofficial projects that were technically challenging and entertaining. (Incidentally, a number of these unofficial projects produced results that were viewed as important and useful to the laboratory.)

We have here two examples of a phenomenon that is common in project management: game playing. It comes in many shapes and sizes. What most project games have in common is players trying to outfox each other or the system. What is troublesome is that the process of outfoxing others entails the manipulation and distortion of information—yet accurate information is important for carrying out projects effectively.

It is equally troublesome that game playing tacitly encourages wholesale dishonesty in projects. For example, in selectively manipulating budget data and distorting schedule data, we are being dishonest. It is easy for this dishonesty to get out of hand. Our initial manipulation may lead to false reports that milestones have been accomplished and deceptive accounts of how project funds have been expended. If the whole project ultimately rests on distortions and lies, we have a good recipe for disaster.

Is game playing to be avoided at all costs? Absolutely not. Frequently it is unavoidable. Sometimes project managers are forced to play system-induced games. Anyone who has worked in an organization governed by seemingly arbitrary fiscal-year budget requirements recognizes that you have to be good at budget games if you want to thrive. Sometimes project managers must play games foisted on them by their bosses (like the boss mentioned earlier who automatically cuts whatever task duration estimate is given him by 20 percent). Sometimes game playing is part of the macho corporate culture, as described in enthralling detail in Kidder's (1981) *Soul of the New Machine*. In this case, if you don't play games—and play them roughly— you are perceived to be some kind of sissy.

While project managers may be forced to play games initiated by others and by the system, they have a choice as to whether they will *initiate* games. For the most part, it is advisable to avoid doing so. As we will see later, in our discussion of project planning and control, project managers should do everything in their power to build their projects on a foundation of accurate and timely information. By playing games, they will be undermining this effort.

Conclusion

People lie at the heart of projects. With white-collar projects, success hinges on people issues. Are our staff committed to the project? Are they intelligent? Do they display initiative when it is needed? Are our bosses supportive? Do they make clear what they expect of us? Do we have good rapport with end-users? Are we dealing with the right set of end-users? Answers to these and related questions give us a good idea of how we will do on our projects.

Many of the issues addressed in this chapter are obvious. We all know that people are multidimensional, that excessive autocracy will lead to the demoralization of creative staff, and that people come in a rich variety of "types." Yet as managers, we too often treat our workers as unidimensional, as if the only important things for them should be their jobs. We too often practice an autocratic management style, feeling threatened by legitimate feedback, which we perceive as unwarranted criticism of our judgments. And we too often pigeonhole people into simplistic types—smart and stupid, cooperative and uncooperative, good and bad.

Thus, for all the obviousness of human relations issues, we find that we inexorably drift away from them in our management practice. It is useful, now and again, to review them carefully.

 **4**

Structuring Project Teams and Building Cohesiveness

Every autumn a certain sports madness overcomes Americans on Sunday afternoons. Week after week, millions of Americans sit in front of their television sets for three or four hours, cheering their favorite football teams, booing the opposing teams, vilifying referees for unfair calls, flicking off their sets when it is obvious that the home team is bound for defeat. For half an hour before the contest, sports commentators examine the players, coaches, and possible game plans in excruciating detail. For half an hour following the contest, they perform postmortems, trying to determine the whys and wherefores of success and defeat. Frequently someone comments that the winning team made a good team effort, while the losing team could not seem to bring things together.

Teams are the basic work unit of sports competition. Similarly, they are the basic work unit of projects. Because of the central role that teams play in projects, it is worthwhile spending some time examining them, to gain a better understanding of what they are and to determine how they contribute to project success and failure. With this knowledge, we can then structure project teams to maximize the likelihood that our projects will be carried out effectively.

Characteristics of Project Teams

A team is a collection of individuals who work together to attain a goal. In order to work together, their individual efforts must be coordinated. In sports, coordination is directed by an all-powerful coach and coaching staff. It is achieved through hours of drills and practice sessions. In projects, we have a fundamentally different perspective on teams, since, as we saw in earlier chapters, project managers are rarely all-powerful and the unique and transitory nature of projects does not make them amenable to repetitive drills.

Project teams, like projects themselves, come in a great variety of shapes and sizes. Some are large, some small. Some must grapple with highly complex problems, others with routine affairs. Some are highly dynamic, with team members constantly changing, while others are stable.

This last point has interesting implications. In sports teams, a large amount of effort is directed at developing team spirit, which requires team members to have a clear image of what the team is and to identify strongly with it. The presence of team spirit may give a team the competitive edge that allows it to win over equally competent teams lacking team spirit. With project teams, however, team members are often borrowed and may have only the briefest exposure to the project effort. They work on a piece of the project, and when they are done they move on to other projects. Because of this, they may not recognize that they are part of a team. Without such recognition, they are incapable of developing team spirit, or what I earlier referred to as project commitment. Of course, from the perspective of the project manager, there *is* a team, whether or not the team members recognize this. The project manager is aware of project goals and knows how the pieces fit together. To the extent that project workers do not realize they are part of a team, however, the project manager's work is more difficult. Clearly, one important task of project managers is the development of some sense of team identification among their staff

Project teams have structure—that is, there are established rules governing the relationships of team members with each other, with the project manager, with the client, and with the product being developed. How the team is structured will have a strong bearing on a project's prospects for success. A well-structured team can enhance the probability of project success, while a poorly structured team will surely lead to trouble. Good team structure is a necessary, though not sufficient, condition for success; poor team structure is a formula for failure.

One question naturally arises: how can we structure the project team in such a way that it will facilitate the effective management of projects? The answer: structure the team to enhance team efficiency.

Team Efficiency

In engineering, the concept of efficiency is straightforward. It is defined as the ratio of output to input. If a device consumes 100 energy units of coal (input) and produces 60 equivalent energy units of electricity (output), we say the device is operating at a level of 60 percent efficiency. With projects, we are unable to measure team input and output precisely, so our treatment of team efficiency is necessarily rough. For purposes of discussion, let us loosely define team efficiency as the fraction of *potential* team performance that is *actually achieved*. Thus, if our team is accomplishing only a small portion of what it could accomplish under ideal circumstances, we say that team efficiency is low. If it is achieving as much as is physically possible, we say that team efficiency is high. Our concern here is not with how to measure team efficiency precisely but with how to achieve it. How can we structure project teams to enhance team efficiency?

To answer this question, it is useful to understand better why systems are inefficient. Mechanical engineers know that two common and interrelated sources of inefficiency in machinery are machine design and friction. If a machine is poorly designed, it will be inefficient. Poor design often means that the machine is not configured in such a way as to minimize the effects of friction. But even a well-designed machine can operate at less than peak efficiency if, through poor maintenance (for example, improper lubrication), it is subject to the effects of friction.

Team efficiency can be viewed analogously. We can say that a project team can be inefficient because its basic design assures inefficiency, and/or because organizational friction keeps it from operating as smoothly as it could. Major structural sources of team inefficiency in projects are matrix-based frictions, poor communication, and poor integration of the efforts of team members. The inefficiencies in each of these cases are interrelated and are rooted in both design inadequacies and organizational friction.

Matrix-Based Frictions

Projects that are heavily dependent on temporarily borrowed staff—that is, projects employing the matrix approach—often have built-in inefficiencies. One important cause of inefficiency in a matrix-structured project is lack of staff continuity. Let's say that Arthur is assigned as a computer programmer/analyst to a project to revamp a hospital's accounts receivable system. He works actively on the project during the early design phase. When the preliminary design is done, he returns to the data processing department, where he is promptly assigned to an office automation project. Two weeks later, top management signs off on the preliminary design and releases funds for a detailed design phase. Since Arthur is working on another project, Linda is assigned as the computer programmer/analyst to the accounts receivable project. Because this is new material for her, she spends her first week simply reviewing overall project requirements, as well as Arthur's specific contributions. Only after this review period is she ready to work actively on the detailed design phase. When this phase is completed, she returns to the data processing department, where she is immediately assigned to a new project. During the implementation phase of the accounts receivable project, still another programmer/analyst is employed. And so on.

It is clear that in this kind of situation, which arises commonly in projects, organizational friction is high, with staff spending substantial time simply reviewing what others before them have done. Couple this with the lack of project commitment characteristic of high-turnover jobs, and it is evident that team efficiency will be low.

Another important matrix-based source of friction is the project manager's lack of direct control over project staff and material resources. Without direct control, it takes more effort and time to acquire needed human and material resources. Project politics may enter the picture, so that acquisition of even a simple piece of equipment may trigger a contorted Rube Goldberg chain of events.

Poor Communication

Information is the lifeblood of projects, and communicating this information effectively to the relevant parties is vital to project success. When communication breaks down, the project is in serious trouble.

There are various kinds of communication-based friction that contribute to team inefficiency. Three will be examined here: communication that becomes an end rather than a means, communication channels that suffer from information arteriosclerosis, and garbled messages that lead to work being done improperly.

Communication as an End Rather Than a Means. As projects become increasingly bureaucratized, proportionately more and more effort is expended on transmitting information and coordinating tasks. On large projects, as much effort may be directed toward communication and coordination as toward carrying out the required tasks. As is illustrated in Figure 4.1, the number of communication channels can grow quadratically as projects become larger. When a project team consists of two members, there is only one communication channel to maintain. When it consists of three members, there are three channels; four members, six channels; five members, ten channels. In general, if the team is comprised of n members, there are potentially $n(n-1)/2$ channels to be maintained. Thus, even a modest team of 20 members has a possible 190 communication channels associated with it! Of course, on most projects not everyone has a need to communicate with everyone else. Nonetheless, the potential exists to overwhelm projects with communication requirements. When an inordinate amount of time is spent sending and receiving messages, team efficiency is bound to decline.

Figure 4.1. Communication Channels.

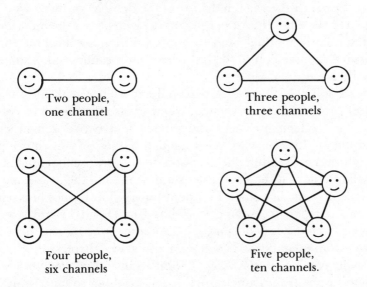

The larger the team, the more communication channels to maintain. In general, n people require $n(n - 1)/2$ communication channels.

Information Atherosclerosis. Atherosclerosis is a condition in which arteries become so clogged that blood can barely trickle through them. Information atherosclerosis occurs when communication channels are so clogged that important information has difficulty making its way through them. The clogging is largely a consequence of requirements that information be processed in a bureaucratically sanctioned fashion. Thus, an important piece of information sent from team member A to team member B may have to pass through five hands before B receives it. Clogging may also be caused by large amounts of useless information floating through channels and blocking the flow of important messages. Here great effort must be expended to separate useful information from chaff.

The principal consequence of information atherosclerosis is that information flows are retarded, contributing to inefficiencies in the team effort.

Garbled Messages. We are all familiar with the parlor game in which ten or fifteen people sit in a line or a circle while someone whispers a message in the ear of the first person, who whispers it in the ear of his or her neighbor, who passes the message to the next individual, and so on. Typically, by the time the message is passed on to the last person, it has undergone some modification.

I still clearly recall a personal experience with message modification. Many years ago, when I was a freshman in college, the college president invited me and two dozen other freshmen to his house for a get-acquainted tea. Upon entering his house, I encountered a reception line of three school officials (the admissions director, the assistant dean, and the dean), and at the end of the line stood President Lowry. I introduced myself to the first person, saying, "Hello, I'm David Frame from Donelson House [my dormitory]." After greeting me, he turned to the woman standing beside him and said, "Professor Jones [or whatever her name was], I want to introduce you to Mr. David Frame from Donelson House." "So nice to meet you," she said. "Are you related to Jim Frame from Schenectady?" I told her I was not, and after a few more seconds of pleasantries she passed me on to the next official in line, introducing me as Jim Frame from Donelson House. This official chatted with me for a moment and then introduced me to President Lowry as Jim Donelson. Over the next four years, whenever I encountered Dr. Lowry on campus he would smile and say, "How do you do, Mr. Donelson?"

This experience illustrates something that frequently occurs in organizations: messages get garbled. The consequences of garbled messages range from neutral to disastrous. In projects, garbled instructions may lead staff to carry out their tasks incorrectly. If their work has to be redone (assuming the mistake is caught), or if their efforts cause spin-off problems with other tasks, team efficiency drops.

My discussion of communication has focused on communication within the project team. It should be noted, however, that communication between the project team and the user of the product emerging from the project is also very important. In particular, if the user's needs are improperly conveyed to the team, the team may produce a deliverable that is rejected and requires rework. This is a very important issue; consequently, I devote a large amount of space to it in Chapters Five and Six.

Poor Integration

As mentioned earlier, one of the basic traits of projects is that they are systems: they are comprised of many interrelated pieces. For the system to work, somehow the pieces have to be brought together and fitted into their proper places. This process of bringing things together is called *systems integration.*

Systems integration is an important function of project managers. They must integrate the pieces of their projects, bringing everything together so that both the project and its product work properly. If integration is not carried out properly, tremendous inefficiencies will be introduced into the project.

Consider, for example, an editor who is compiling a handbook on gardening. The handbook will contain twenty-five chapters, each written by a recognized expert. If the editor does not carefully spell out what she expects of each of the authors—if she does not take steps to integrate the pieces into a whole—she will have a hodgepodge of chapters turned in to her. Some will be long, some short. Some will be narrated in a very folksy manner; others will be rigidly academic in tone. Some will be filled with footnotes; others will lack any references to related material. Many will repeat material covered in other chapters.

Ultimately, if the editor wants a work that hangs together nicely, she will either have to return the chapter manuscripts to the authors, with instructions on how to revise them so that they dovetail with each other, or she and her staff will have to spend enormous amounts of time editing and rewriting the submitted material. In any event, a poor initial effort at integrating the separate chapters into a cohesive book will cause burdensome rework and will yield low levels of team efficiency on the project.

This matter of integration is especially crucial in software development projects. In developing complex software, programmers typically work separately on different pieces of the system. Major problems often arise when attempts are later made to integrate the pieces into a whole. What happens, using the jargon of systems analysis, is that "bugs arise at the interfaces." Simply put, while the pieces may be internally consistent and bug-free, they don't quite fit together, leading the system to malfunction. A great deal of time and effort must be dedicated to trying to get the pieces to fit together. More time is usually spent testing and debugging the system to ensure integration than writing lines of computer code.

To the extent that project managers are effective systems integrators, they dramatically increase the efficiency of their project teams.

Structuring Teams

Because we want to structure project teams in such a way that the structure enhances team efficiency, we clearly want to avoid structures that encourage the organizational and design frictions just discussed. Thus, a desirable project team structure is one that copes with staff turnover and lack of direct project manager control over resources, enhances effective communication among project team members, and facilitates the integration of the many pieces of the project.

There is no one structure that fits the bill for all projects. A structure that is ideal for one project may fail dismally with another. Various things must be taken into account in configuring a team structure. What is the size of the project? Can staff be permanently assigned to it, or will there be high levels of staff turnover? What is the technical nature of the project? What is the corporate culture like? What are the psychological characteristics of the team members and other relevant project actors?

To illustrate team structure considerations concretely, we will examine the consequences of structuring a hypothetical project in four different ways. The project is a common one faced by professional consultants—to write a technical report on some topic of interest to a client.

Isomorphic Team Structure. The adjective *isomorphic* comes from the Greek *iso*, which means equal or same, and *morph*, which means form or shape. Two things are isomorphic when they share the same structural appearance.

If we configure a project team so that it closely reflects the physical structure of the deliverable—the thing that is being produced—the team and the deliverable are isomorphic in respect to each other. In Figure 4.2, I illustrate an isomorphic team configuration for our project to write a technical report for a client. Figure 4.2a shows what the report will look like, a simple document with five chapters. Figure 4.2b shows how the team can be configured to match the structure of the deliverable. The project manager corresponds to the fully integrated report, while each of five team members corresponds to one of the report's five chapters.

Figure 4.2. Isomorphic Team Structure.

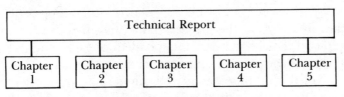

4.2a. Structure of the Deliverable.

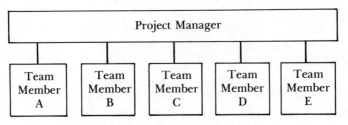

4.2b. Structure of the Project Team.

With a project structured this way, there is always a real risk that the pieces (the chapters in our example) will not fit together nicely, since each is being developed independently. Clearly, then, a major function of project managers is to serve as integrators. They must interact closely and continually with their staff to make sure that staff members produce pieces that will fit in the final product. In our specific example, the project manager should focus on maintaining a consistent writing style among his or her workers, avoiding duplication in the material being covered in the different chapters, and linking together the material through cross-references between the chapters. One way he or she can accomplish this integration is to hold weekly staff meetings at which team members briefly describe their efforts and compare notes.

There are several advantages to the isomorphic approach. For one thing, it is organizationally simple. Team structure simply follows the structure of the deliverable. Each team member is responsible for developing one or more pieces of the deliverable. If progress on one chapter of the report begins to lag seriously, the project manager immediately knows whom to talk to in order to find out what the problem is.

Second, if the different modules of the system are independent, the isomorphic approach allows parallel implementation of tasks, which may considerably shorten the amount of time it takes to carry out the project. Thus, in our technical report example, if the chapters are independent of each other, all five chapters can be written simultaneously.

Third, this approach is well suited to projects where new staff members are getting their first exposure to a project management environment. Its simplicity eases novices into their new jobs, rather than overwhelming them with complexity. Furthermore, the project manager can take on the role of mentor to the new staff, watching over them closely and providing them with important guidance on how projects are carried out in the organization.

In general, the isomorphic approach can be highly effective in dealing with projects on which the different pieces that make up the deliverable are relatively independent of each other.

In such cases, problems of systems integration are much smaller than in projects on which the pieces are inextricably tied together.

   Specialty Team Structure. The specialty approach to structuring teams is illustrated in Figure 4.3. With the specialty approach, team members may be asked to apply their special expertise across a wide array of tasks. In this case, the project workers' orientation is toward their specialty rather than toward a specific deliverable.

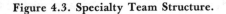

Figure 4.3. Specialty Team Structure.

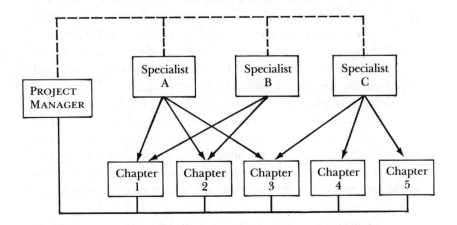

   With a specialty structure, coordination of staff efforts becomes complex, since staff work is distributed across many tasks. Typically, project staff focus on a small piece of the deliverable without an appreciation of how that piece fits into the larger system. Their clear-cut responsibility toward a given deliverable disappears. Responsibility is now more diffuse, and it may be difficult to diagnose the cause of the problem if something goes wrong.

   Because the specialty approach fractionates work along functional lines, project managers must pay particular attention to keeping track of the diverse piecemeal efforts and making sure that they will ultimately fit together. Problems with integration are greater here than with the isomorphic approach. Not only do we want to integrate the different chapters so that they fit together, but we must also focus on integrating the work of different people within each chapter. Similarly, the need to maintain good communication is greater, particularly in view of the fact that staff are likely to be wearing specialty blinders and therefore be unaware of and possibly uninterested in the big picture.

One advantage of the specialty approach is that it capitalizes on staff expertise and specialization of labor. The people doing the project work are not amateurs; they should know what they're doing. Another advantage of this approach is that it fits in nicely with a matrix system. Staff can be borrowed from functional departments and assigned work on different tasks. When they have finished their work, they can return to their functional departments for reassignment to other projects. Of course, as I mentioned earlier, various sources of team friction that arise in matrix approaches reduce team efficiency. However, matrix management is a fact of life for many project workers. Project managers who work in an organization that employs matrix management should give serious attention to structuring project teams according to the specialties of the team members.

Egoless Team Structure. Back in the early 1970s, Gerald Weinberg noted in *The Psychology of Computer Programming* that a major cause of problems in computer programming projects is the ego of computer programmers. They are often more interested in developing tour-de-force programs than in doing what is necessary to come up with a well-integrated product. Too often they are not good team players. In order to deal with this common problem, Weinberg suggested that project teams should be structured to minimize the ill effects of egos. When we look at the product of an egoless team, the results of a truly collaborative effort, it should be difficult to determine who produced what portion of the product.

The structure of a three-person egoless team is shown in

Figure 4.4. Note that there is no obvious leader on the egoless team. Decisions are achieved through consensus, and project tasks often reflect the input of all the team members. For example, in our technical report case, Martha may write a draft of the first chapter and then turn it over to George, who edits and reworks it. After all the chapters are done, Miriam may do a final editing of the report, to make sure that it is well integrated. To the extent that team members collaborate jointly like this, problems of ego will be minimized.

Figure 4.4. Egoless Team Structure.

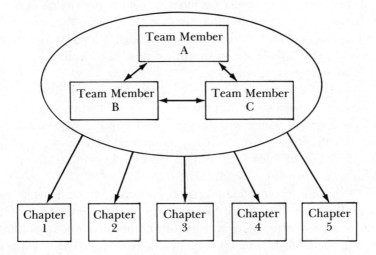

The egoless team structure encourages high levels of interactivity and communication among project members. They are continually in touch with each other and make decisions through consensus. If communication is good, and if team members are working together toward a common goal, problems of systems integration should be low.

I have heard many scathing criticisms of the egoless team approach by those who have tried to implement it in their organizations. One of the most common is that "the egoless team doesn't work, because *people have egos.*" Project workers—especially those with great talent—possess pride of authorship. They want to make their unique contributions, to stand out from the crowd, and they strongly resist attempts to downplay their egos. Another criticism focuses on the lack of leadership on egoless teams. "Without strong leadership, there is a tendency for egoless teams to drift, " comments one project manager who worked in a company that espoused the egoless approach to team structure.

To those who declare that egoless teams go against human nature (and I often hear this comment), I point out that in Asian cultures, with their stress on harmony and consensus, egoless teams are more the rule than the exception. The Western concept of leadership, based on individualism, is alien to the East. Consider the Japanese dictum that states "The nail that stands up is hammered down."

My feeling is that egoless teams can work effectively in Western cultures in certain situations. First, team size must be relatively small, since with larger teams communication channels proliferate, leading to bureaucracy and its attendant inefficiencies. Furthermore, with large teams it becomes difficult to achieve a meaningful consensus.

Second, egoless teams require continuity in team membership. They are very much like a sports team in this respect. On television recently, there was a story about a college basketball team that had four starting players who were brothers. "I spend most of my time trying to get team members used to playing with each other," said the coach. "These brothers have been playing together a whole lifetime. They're remarkable." As with sports teams, team efficiency on egoless teams is highly dependent on the team members' knowing each other's operating styles, technical capabilities, weaknesses, and so on. This knowledge can develop only if staff work together continually. You cannot have egoless teams functioning effectively as a matrix.

Third, egoless teams may function well on ill-defined state-of-the-art projects for which the final deliverable is at first only vaguely conceived. Basic research projects typically have these characteristics. A synergistic team (one on which the effectiveness of the combined team is greater than the effectiveness of the individual team members) may be able to pool the talents of the team members and come up with creative solutions that the team members could not achieve if working alone.

Finally, egoless teams may be effective on projects where highly creative team members resist the imposition of strong leadership, which goes against their grain and which, they feel, restricts creativity.

Surgical Team Structure. Frederick P. Brooks, in his classic work on managing software projects, *The Mythical Man-Month* (1975), promotes use of an approach he calls the surgical team. (In software project management, this approach, developed originally by Harlan Mills of IBM, is called the chief programmer team concept.) Brooks asks us to consider how a surgical team functions. At the heart of the team is the surgeon, who actually performs the surgery on the patient. The surgeon is surrounded by assistants—an anesthesiologist, nurses, interns—who provide him or her with all manner of assistance. In the final analysis, however, it is the surgeon who actually carries out the surgical procedure. He or she calls the shots. The primary function of the assistants is to help the surgeon carry out his task most effectively, with *the surgeon defining effectiveness.*

One fundamental objective of the surgical approach in medicine is to allow the surgeon to pursue his work freely, unencumbered by administrative and technical obligations. The surgeon's task is to perform surgery. Billing of the patient can be handled by administrative staff, anesthesia can be administered by an anesthesiologist, surgical tools can be maintained by the nursing staff, examination of removed tissue can be carried out by a pathologist, and so on. Similarly, in project management one individual is given total responsibility for carrying out the main body of project work while being shielded from administrative paper pushing.

The surgical approach to team structure stands in diametrical opposition to the egoless approach. With the surgical approach, all attention focuses on a single individual and his or her abilities. With the egoless approach, it is the overall group effort that counts.

Figure 4.5 shows how the surgical approach can be applied to our project to write a technical report. A chief writer stands at the heart of the undertaking. This individual will write

Figure 4.5. Surgical Team Approach.

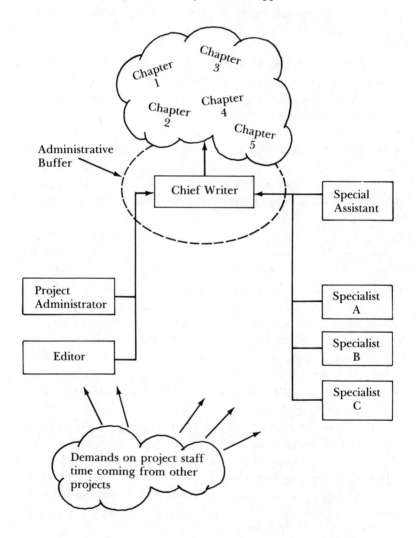

the whole technical report. She has been chosen for this position because she writes quickly and clearly and understands the technical content of the study. She is buffered from administrative concerns by an administrative staff member, who keeps track of hours devoted to the project, progress reports, and the like. She is relieved of editorial burdens by an editorial staff member, who at the end of each day reads her writing, corrects misspellings and grammatical errors, spots and removes minor factual inconsistencies, and so on. In addition, she is provided with technical back-up, individuals who are specialists on the material covered in the technical report. If at any point she needs detailed information on a particular topic, she will confer with the appropriate specialist to obtain this information.

At her side is her special assistant, an alter ego who is also a good writer, though perhaps with less experience. The special assistant plays numerous roles. For example, he may serve as an intermediary between the chief writer and the specialists. His most significant role, however, is to keep fully abreast of what the chief writer has done and to take over the project if necessary. The special assistant is an insurance policy against what in project management is called the Mack truck syndrome, which gets its name from the question "What happens to the project if on the way to work the project manager gets hit by a Mack truck?"

A major advantage of the surgical team approach is that it tackles head-on the issue of systems integration. Since project output flows from the mind of a single individual, the pieces being produced are likely to fit together nicely. Stylistic and factual inconsistencies and duplication of effort will be minimized. The final product will be well integrated.

Another advantage is that the surgical approach can be readily adapted to matrix organizations. This can be seen in Figure 4.5, which shows that functional specialists serve as a central information pool that can be used by a number of projects.

One disadvantage of the surgical approach is that it requires a superlatively capable individual to play the role of surgeon. If such an individual is not available, the resulting product may be mediocre.

Another disadvantage is that the surgical team may end up with three bosses. The surgeon is clearly a boss, but principally in regard to technical matters. The administrative chief is a boss in the sense that he or she is in charge of maintaining and controlling budgets, schedules, and material resource allocations. Finally, the special assistant may assume responsibility for coordinating and controlling the technical personnel who serve as project specialists. If these three individuals do not communicate with each other clearly and frequently, or if they hold differing perceptions of project goals, team efficiency will be low.

The surgical team approach is most effective on design projects, computer coding projects, and projects—such as our technical report project—that entail large amounts of writing. Brooks claims that it is also an effective approach on very large projects where each project module is given a surgical team structure. When used in this way, according to Brooks, this approach combines small-project efficiency and consistency with large-project scope.

This discussion of four approaches to structuring a project team is not meant to be exhaustive. Many other approaches can be undertaken. Rather, it is illustrative. It shows that—for a single project to write a technical report—team structure has a dramatic impact on the way in which a project is carried out. It also shows that there is no one perfect structure for managing projects. An approach that addresses the issue of systems integration (the surgical team) may lead to confusion as to who is in charge. An approach that fosters intense and open communication among team tembers (the egoless team) may suffer from lack of leadership. An approach that is conceptually simple and straightforward (the isomorphic team) may yield systems integration problems. And an approach that dovetails nicely in a matrix environment (the specialist team) may have associated with it all the problems that can come with matrix management.

Creating Team Identification

The focus of the discussion up until now has been on the mechanical aspects of putting a team together. Beyond mechanics, there is the question of creating a sense of team cohesion among the team members. The problem is that people working on projects are typically on loan and have little opportunity or motivation to develop a commitment toward the projects. It is clearly in the interest of project managers to stimulate a sense of project identity among workers attached to their projects.

There are many ways in which they can do this. What sometimes pulls a team together is the personality and special management style of the project manager, or his or her expertise. Charismatic managers or those with a legendary reputation for technical prowess easily catch the attention of their staff, who recognize that they are privileged to work with these managers.

Those of us lacking exceptional charismatic or technical prowess must work hard at developing a sense of project identity among project staff. Among the steps that can be taken to do this, three are almost universally useful: use staff meetings effectively, employ quality circles, and employ task forces.

Use Staff Meetings Effectively. Staff meetings are the bane of many information-age workers. They are often perceived as time killers, intrusions that interrupt the flow of productive work. Staff meetings often deserve the poor reputation they have: frequently bosses simply mount their soapboxes and spout opinions on the state of the world to a captive audience. This is too bad, since these meetings, when carried out effectively, serve two important functions. One obvious function is to convey information to and among staff members. It is at staff meetings that new policy directions are conveyed to workers and that staff have the opportunity to coordinate their efforts with each other.

A more important function of these meetings, from the perspective of team building, is to provide staff with a sense of team identity. The staff meeting is a physical embodiment of the team. Project staff who otherwise work alone or drift into and out of a particular project see that there is substance to the team and that they are part of a larger unit. If the meetings are pleasant experiences and well run, staff will develop a sense that the project itself is being carried out effectively.

Project managers should take staff meetings seriously, not treat them in an offhand manner. A large share of the image that team members have of the competence and management ability of their project managers will be garnered at these meetings. If the meetings are boring and disorganized, it is natural to assume that the project manager is likewise boring and disorganized. If the meetings are fast-moving and open, and if they signal a willingness to act upon the views of all project workers, the foundation has been laid for developing team cohesion on the project.

Employ Quality Circles. Quality circles are regular gatherings of small groups of workers to discuss ways of improving work performance. A typical group is comprised of ten or fewer people who meet regularly for one or two hours once a month. In these meetings, they identify problems they encounter in their work, offer solutions to these problems, and review the effectiveness of past attempts to improve work performance.

The basic rationale for having quality circles is twofold. First, those actually doing the work are in a good position to see how the work can be done even better. Second, by involving workers in decision making, management enhances worker commitment to doing a good job. In projects, quality circles serve an important additional function: they are good instruments for enhancing team identification. When quality circles are used on projects, team members who would normally have little or no contact with each other get to sit down together and work jointly to improve project performance. Like the oarsmen in a shell, they may develop a feeling that team performance will be strengthened if they all pull together.

Project managers who want to employ quality circles on their projects will have to take the initiative in setting them up, since it is unlikely that project staff who come from different parts of the organization and are working only temporarily on the project will spontaneously organize themselves into such circles. Project managers should also demonstrate a willingness to meet frequently with the groups and to follow their recommendations when appropriate.

Employ Task Forces. Task forces serve much the same team-building function as quality circles. However, whereas quality circles meet regularly and deal with across-the-board issues, task forces focus on a specific problem and meet as often as necessary to resolve the problem. One profitable use of task forces is for needs/requirements definition on a project. In the development of a hardware or software system, for example, system designers, analysts, implementers, and testers can get together in a task force with end-users to define and articulate end-user needs and system requirements. Not only will this approach lead to a superior statement of needs and requirements, but it will also contribute to a stronger sense of team identity among project workers who would otherwise not interact with each other.

What is appealing about these three suggestions for creating team identification on projects is that they are relatively easy to implement and, if carried out properly, will produce results. They are only the tip of the iceberg, however; many other approaches can be employed as well. For example, on larger, more structured projects, awards can be offered for exemplary performance, competitions can be established to motivate different groups to perform better than their colleagues, and after-work social activities can be organized for members of the project team. The important thing here is recognition that most project situations do not automatically create a sense of team identification among project workers. Project managers must consciously strive to create this sense if they want to run projects peopled by highly motivated and effective workers *who care* whether the project is carried out in the best manner possible.

Conclusion

Projects are carried out through teams, but these teams are typically fragmented and poorly defined, owing to the exigencies of matrix management. An important function of project managers is to consciously create a team structure where no discernible structure exists. This is not trivial, since there are countless ways teams can be organized. One prime consideration in structuring a team should be to select a structure that enhances team efficiency.

It is not enough simply to select an appropriate team structure, however. Team members must be encouraged to identify with the team, to develop team spirit, and to do what is necessary to make the project succeed. The problem is that team members are usually on temporary loan to the project and have little stake in whether it succeeds or fails. Project managers must create a sense of identity in an environment that does little to encourage cohesiveness. They must make stakeholders out of their staff. They can do this through a number of ways, including the skillful use of staff meetings and the employment of quality circles and task forces.

5

Making Certain
a Project Is Based
on a Clear Need

It may be recalled that this book looks at project management from the perspective of the pitfalls that project managers are likely to encounter. The purpose of focusing on pitfalls is not to accentuate the negative and thereby discourage people from assuming project management responsibilities. Rather, it is to introduce a strong dose of reality into the project management process. The road traveled by project managers is littered with potholes and debris. You can count on it! This does not mean that the road is impassable, however. Many of the problems that project managers encounter are created by the very nature of the project management process and human organization. They are predictable and can be anticipated. With foreknowledge of pitfalls, project managers can avoid them or mitigate their harmful effects. At the very least, unpleasant surprises can be minimized.

In the previous three chapters, we concentrated on identifying and dealing with organizationally rooted problems. Now we turn our attention toward identifying and resolving problems associated with the formulation of end-user needs (this chapter) and the specification of project requirements (next chapter).

103

Evolution of Needs

Projects arise in order to meet human needs. A need emerges and is recognized, and then management determines whether the need is worth fulfilling. If it is, a project is organized to satisfy the need. Thus, needs are the fundamental driving force behind projects. This seminal aspect of needs makes them important for project management. Their emergence sets off the whole project process, and if at the outset we do not fully understand a need and its implications, if we incorrectly articulate it, or if we mistakenly address the wrong need, we have gotten off to a bad start and can be certain that our project will be trouble-filled.

Needs evolve from something very amorphous to something well structured and clearly understood. The following case study illustrates how needs evolve.

RALPH'S DRUGSTORE. Ralph's Drugstore is located in a small midwestern town. While visiting Minneapolis on vacation, Ralph Amdahl, the drugstore's owner, was impressed by the volume of business carried out by the city's discount drugstores. Upon returning home, he converted his drugstore into a discount operation, a complicated process that took six months.

Business volume soon increased dramatically. People would come from miles away to take advantage of Ralph's discount prices. The store aisles were constantly jammed, and a long line snaked from the store's single cash register. Ralph witnessed the crowds with mixed emotions. On the one hand, it was good to see that his new discount policy was bringing in the crowds. On the other hand, customer dissatisfaction was growing. Complaints were primarily directed at three things: the crowded conditions in the store, stockouts of special sale items, and long waits in the checkout line. Ralph was concerned that his success would backfire and that customer dissatisfaction with service would stymie growth.

Ralph expressed his concerns to Marie, his wife and business partner. One evening, the two of them sat down after dinner to discuss the future of the business. They determined that although their discount business was dramatically different from their previous opera-

tion, the basic way they conducted their business had not changed. For example, the physical layout of the store was no different than it had been before, and it was now apparent that this layout was inadequate to deal with the growth in customer traffic. Ralph and Marie decided that they needed more floor space, more shelf space, more cash registers, and more sales staff. They would have to either remodel their current facilities, build new facilities, or rent different facilities. With paper and pencil, they roughly calculated their requirements: to meet anticipated customer traffic, they would need to double floor space and shelf space and add at least two cash registers. They concluded that to satisfy these requirements they would have to move to new facilities.

At this point, they met twice with a local architect to identify how best to configure a store to make it better suited to the new kind of business they were doing. Using the information garnered from these meetings, the architect designed three different store configurations. Ralph and Marie were excited by the second design, which required them to build rather than rent a new structure; and, after suggesting some minor modifications to the plan, they authorized the architect to proceed to make detailed drawings of the new facility. He completed the architectural plans within six weeks, and three months later groundbreaking for the new store was initiated.

The Needs/Requirements Life Cycle

The case of Ralph's Drugstore illustrates the evolution of needs from something vague and nascent to something quite tangible that serves as the basis of a project plan. First, there is a *needs emergence phase:* customer traffic at Ralph's Drugstore increased dramatically after Ralph converted his store into a discount operation, and this growth in traffic led to a number of problems. Then there is a *needs recognition phase:* Ralph became aware that his facilities could not adequately handle the increase in customer traffic. This is followed by a *needs articulation phase:* Ralph and Marie consciously addressed the perceived need and attempted to describe its boundaries and implications.

After the needs have been articulated, they can serve as the basis for establishing *functional requirements*—a narrative description of what a project would have to do if it were to meet the articulated needs. In the case of Ralph's Drugstore, functional requirements emerged from Ralph's and Marie's discussions with the architect. From these functional requirements, the architect was able to articulate *technical requirements* (for example, blueprints), around which a project plan to build a new facility would be structured.

Because needs are the driving force behind projects, it is useful to examine these different phases of the needs/requirements life cycle in more detail.

Needs Emergence. Change is the generator of needs. With the status quo, needs remain constant; with change, new needs emerge and old ones fall away. Because we live in an age characterized by change, we face the continual emergence of new needs.

Needs can arise from within or outside an organization. Internal needs are typically related to improving organizational performance. An agency overwhelmed with paperwork may have a strong need to reduce paperwork. A company periodically facing the prospect of worker strikes may have a need to improve management-employee relations. A law office establishing branches in different cities will have a need to communicate effectively with these branches.

Organizations are also vitally interested in needs arising in the environment outside the organization. These environmentally generated needs are the lifeblood of for-profit companies. Emerging needs for more powerful computing capabilities, better-tasting TV dinners, harder drill bits, more durable handbags, and so on, are what keep companies in business and drive them to innovate. Environmentally generated needs are also important to nonprofit and governmental organizations. The growing need of individuals to avoid having obsolete skills is what enables universities to thrive. The whole rationale of organizations such as the Red Cross is to respond to needs created by natural disasters, such as floods and fires. Similarly, government—the servant of the people—is predicated on addressing societal needs.

Needs Recognition. It is not enough simply to have needs emerge. These needs must be recognized for what they are. If they are not seen to exist, no action will be undertaken to satisfy them. This is an obvious point, yet the recognition of needs is not a trivial matter. It is not easy to spot emerging needs. Often we are so accustomed to doing things in a given way that we do not see that as things change new needs emerge; we fail to notice that the old ways of doing things may no longer be effective.

The transistor, developed as a substitute for the vacuum tube, is a case in point. The U.S. military underwrote the considerable expense of developing transistors because they had a need for components more reliable than vacuum tubes in military hardware. Thus, the commercial development of transistors was largely a response to military needs. American manufacturers only vaguely perceived new applications of transistors to meet consumer needs. The Japanese, however, saw how transistors could lead to miniaturization of electronic devices, and they further saw how miniaturization could satisfy consumer needs to, say, take a radio on a picnic or to the beach. This recognition of consumer needs for portable electronic devices launched Japan on its enormously successful journey into the realm of consumer electronics.

Recognition of needs requires conscious effort. People in organizations must constantly ask, What are our needs? What are the needs of our clients (consumers, taxpayers, victims of disaster, students, and so on)? Procedures must be established for systematically identifying needs. The information resource management department in an organization may hold monthly meetings to identify newly emerging information needs within the organization. The marketing department may require its sales force to submit a brief statement of their perceptions of client needs each time they meet with a client. A municipal government may establish a liaison office to obtain feedback from citizens on their needs.

Attention must focus not only on existing needs but on anticipated needs as well. Thus, effective needs recognition requires *forecasting*. This forecasting can be very simple. For example, a department manager can meet with three or four staff members once a month and, through a one- or two-hour brainstorming session, develop ideas of what future needs might be. Or the forecasting can be elaborate, entailing the building of quantitative models that will predict future conditions. The important thing is not the degree of sophistication of the forecasting effort but the fact that a conscious effort is being undertaken to anticipate the future emergence of needs.

Needs Articulation. After a need is recognized, it must be clearly articulated. Needs articulation entails an in-depth scrutiny of the recognized need. With such a scrutiny, our understanding of the need will change. Too often we accept needs at face value and lose sight of the reality that lies beneath the surface. We are overwhelmed with paper in our office, and we immediately jump to the conclusion that we should computerize in order to create a paperless office. The quality of our products is declining, so we conclude that we need more inspectors to examine the products for defects. In both instances, we have zeroed in on superficial needs. In most office environments that are drowning in paper, the need is not for computers but for better information management procedures. In production environments where quality is a problem, the need is not for more inspectors, who catch defects only *after* they occur, but for new processes that will actually reduce the number of defects. In other words, if we thoroughly examine a particular need, we are less likely to grab onto the superficial. Often the very act of trying to describe something precisely gives us a better understanding of what we are looking at.

Needs articulation has a practical side to it. It serves as the basis for the development of functional requirements. What this means is that after a need has been clearly articulated—that is, after it has been fully and unambiguously stated—we can go about the business of stipulating in concrete terms what we have to do in order to achieve it. Obviously, if we have done a poor job of articulating the need, our functional requirements will be misdirected and the resulting project will be nonresponsive to the true need.

In practice, needs can be articulated in a number of different ways. One approach to effectively articulating needs is to carry out the following five steps:

Step 1: Ask those who have the need to define it as clearly as possible. It is important to see the need through the end-users' eyes, even though at this point they usually have only the vaguest notion of what that need is. Individuals with a need usually have a *feeling* for the need rather than a solid grasp of what it is. Frequently they cannot precisely articulate their need because they are too close to it and lack the technical competence to do so. While it is important to determine how end-users view their needs, you should not accept these views at face value.

Step 2: Ask a full set of questions about the need. It is wise to maintain a set of stock questions to ask when you are trying to articulate needs precisely. These questions should force you to address the needs from different perspectives. When answered, they will give you a multidimensional view of the needs. Pertinent questions include:

- How do those having the need define it?
- Is the need real? Is this need the true need, or is it masking a more basic need?
- Can we resolve the need? Can someone else resolve it? Is it resolvable at all?
- Is the need important? Is it worth trying to satisfy?
- What are the implications of the need? If fulfilled, will it give rise to other needs? By satisfying it, will we also be satisfying other needs? Does the emerging need replace an existing need?
- Who are the actors that are most directly touched by the need? Do they agree that it is a worthwhile need? How will satisfaction of the need affect them? How will they react to efforts to satisfy it?
- How does the need affect my organization? How does it affect me?

Step 3: Carry out whatever research is necessary to enable you to understand the need better. Before you can properly articulate a need, you must understand it in all of its aspects, including those that are technical. How can we adequately formulate needs to enhance the productivity of the office, for example, if we are ignorant of present and potential office technologies? You may carry out research on the technical aspects of the need within your organization; or, if your organization lacks sufficient expertise, you can tap the expertise of outside consultants.

Step 4: In view of insights gained in the first three steps, formulate the need as best you can. At this point, you have a far better grasp of the need and its implications than you did at the outset. When you formulate the need now, it will probably look much different than it initially did.

Step 5: Ask the end-users to respond to your formulation of the need, and revise your formulation accordingly. One widely recognized pitfall in needs formulation is that the needs eventually articulated are not those of the end-user whose needs are supposedly being addressed but, rather, are those of the professionals who are trying to articulate the needs on behalf of the end-user. During the needs/requirements life cycle, it is common for experts to modify needs so that they satisfy the experts but not the end-user. The problem here is obvious: the ultimate product that is created on the basis of the modified needs will probably be underutilized, misutilized, or not utilized at all by the end-user. In order to reduce the likelihood of this happening, the needs formulator should make a great effort to be sure that what he or she has articulated does indeed reflect end-users' needs. This can be done by working closely with end-users, getting their reactions to the newly articulated needs, and revising the needs statement to reflect end-user desires.

Functional and Technical Requirements. After needs have been carefully defined, we can use them as the basis for developing a project plan. We do this by formulating the needs as functional requirements. Functional requirements describe the characteristics of the deliverable—what emerges from the project—in ordinary, nontechnical language. They are written so that nontechnical people can understand them. A functional requirement flowing from a school's need to improve the mathematics abilities of its sixth graders might be stated as follows: "We want to have 95 percent of our sixth graders scoring in the top six deciles of the Smith-Jones Mathematics Achievement Test by the end of the next academic year."

Technical requirements then emerge from the functional requirements. Although functional requirements should be clearly stated, they typically do not offer enough precise guidance for project staff to use them as targets for guiding their efforts. While functional requirements are designed to assure that end-users know what they are getting out of a project, technical requirements are written for the technical staff. Consequently, technical requirements are often incomprehensible to the end-user, who lacks the training to know what they mean. In a hypothethical software project, the functional requirements may stipulate that a data base system will be developed to allow access to financial data through a remote terminal; the corresponding technical requirements would spell out the architecture of the data structure, the language in which the data base management system will be written, the hardware on which the system will run, telecommunication protocols that should be used, and so forth.

The effective specification of requirements is one of the most challenging undertakings project planners and managers face. Inadequately specified requirements will guarantee poor project results. (I address requirements in detail in the next chapter, so I will postpone discussing characteristics of well-stated requirements and the problems associated with their formulation until then.)

Pitfalls in Defining Needs

The earlier discussion of the needs/requirements life cycle hinted that there are many ways in which the process of defining needs can go awry. Some of the problems in defining needs are subtle; we may not even realize we have a problem until our project starts to unravel. It is worthwhile exploring common pitfalls that arise in defining needs, so that we are alerted to their existence and are prepared to deal with them. Three broad categories of problems are examined here: problems with inherently fuzzy needs, problems with identifying solutions before needs have been fully defined, and problems with addressing the needs of the wrong end-users.

Dealing with Inherently Fuzzy Needs

The most fundamental cause of difficulties in defining needs is their inherent fuzziness. When needs first emerge, they are rough and ill-defined, just a glimmer of an idea. They represent something new, something different. The more unique they are, the greater their imprecision. Their articulation is undertaken iteratively. At first they are only vaguely perceived; after we address them systematically and refine them, they gradually take on shape and substance. Two related characteristics of needs contribute to their natural fuzziness: needs are dynamic, and needs are rarely understood by end-users.

Dynamic Needs. Needs are dynamic and ever changing. One project manager told me that articulating needs is like shooting at a moving target. Another, choosing a more colorful metaphor, described it as trying to nail jelly to the wall. The reason for this dynamic nature of needs is that they are defined in relation to the environment in which they emerge. In our Ralph's Drugstore case study, for example, increases in customer traffic resulted in a need for Ralph to initiate some fundamental changes in the way he did business. Unfortunately, as needs emerge and we wrestle to articulate them precisely, the environment does not stand still but continues to change. No doubt by the time Ralph's new drugstore opens, the needs it was designed to serve will have changed somewhat and new needs will have emerged.

How can project planners and managers cope with this ever-changing character of needs? For one thing, they can recognize that it exists. They should avoid casting needs statements in concrete as if they were immutable. Beyond this, they should be aware that the changing nature of needs may require changes in the project plan once project implementation has begun. Given the dynamic nature of needs, it is a good idea to create flexible project plans.

Something else project planners and managers can do is to anticipate changes in needs through forecasting. In articulating a need, they should define it not only in terms of the existing environment but in the context of an anticipated future environment as well. This is difficult to do. It is hard enough to get a handle on existing needs; it is much harder to articulate needs that don't exist now and may never exist.

Misunderstood Needs. End-users generally operate according to the dictum "I'm not sure what I want, but I'll know it when I see it." While they have a *sense* of their needs, they may not fully understand them and their implications. Their ill-defined perceptions of their needs are likely to shift with the slightest change in circumstances. This is not to say that their needs are not real. They *are* real. However, they are only vaguely perceived, and they cannot be satisfied effectively as long as they are conceived in their current form. The implications of all this for project planners are clear: if managers base their plans solely on end-user statements of needs, they are not likely to produce deliverables that will satisfy the end-users' true needs.

Newcomers to project management are often frustrated in their dealings with end-users, because they see them as wishy-washy and a bit dense in the skull—individuals who don't know what they want and are never satisfied with what they get. This attitude will invariably lead to an us-versus-them mentality that will undermine project effectiveness. Project staff must recognize that one significant role they play is guide to end-users. Working closely with end-users, project staff must help them to identify clearly what it is they need. Project staff will derive benefits from such an approach in at least two ways. First, by working closely with end-users, they will be better able to plan a project whose deliverables actually address user needs. Second, end-user involvement in the needs articulation effort will educate them about the nature and implications of their needs, and will increase their commitment to using the project's deliverables.

Identifying Solutions Prematurely

The inherent fuzziness of needs is clearly a major pitfall facing project planners. Another common pitfall is shortcutting the needs articulation process, causing us to come up with answers before we have formulated the right questions.

Performing an analysis of needs requires a good deal of patience and self-control. From the moment we first perceive the existence of a need, ideas enter our heads on how to satisfy it. Frequently we are ready to offer a solution before we fully understand the need. This is illustrated in the following case:

AN EDIFICE COMPLEX. The dean of an urban engineering school determines that the school's physical plant—its administrative offices, faculty offices, classrooms, and laboratories—is decaying and no longer meets the needs of the faculty and student body. He decides that what the engineering school needs is a brand-new physical plant—a six-story building that will cost $50 million to build. He and his staff begin a major three-year drive to raise the money necessary to build the new facility.

When news of the dean's plans leaks out to the engineering faculty, some professors express concern about the building project. One wag jokingly talks about the dean's "edifice complex." They recognize that the current facilities are in bad shape, and they all would like to have more posh accommodations. However, they see the investment in a new plant as increasing the school's operating costs, which translates into higher tuition for students at a time when tuition rates are already astronomical. If the new plant is built, it seems inevitable that the engineering school will price itself out of the market.

A consensus emerges among these faculty members that the school should be pursuing avenues that will enhance the teaching and research environment and at the same time contribute to a decrease in tuition. When the associate dean hears about this view, he says, "That doesn't sound like much of a suggestion to me. How can we simultaneously build a first-rate facility and reduce tuition? The problem is that these teachers want to have their cake and eat it too."

The divergence in outlook held by the dean and the dissenting faculty is explained by the ways in which they identify the engineering school's needs. The dean walks through the existing facilities and sees plaster falling off the walls, peeling paint, ancient blackboards, linoleum flooring that has completely worn through in spots, professors' offices that are dingy and underheated. His conclusion: "What we need at the engineering school is new facilities." He may be right; he may be wrong. What is important to note is that his expression of the school's need has embedded in it the solution to the need. The solution, of course, is to build new facilities. Other possible solutions have been shut out.

The dissenting engineering faculty members have a different perspective. They are concerned that the building program will ultimately lead to a loss of students, which in turn may lead to the loss of teaching jobs. Their perception of the school's need: "We must enhance teaching and research, and also assure that the school is affordable for engineering students." No obvious solutions are inherent in this statement of needs. The construction of new facilities may satisfy the need, as might refurbishing the old facilities, initiating an electronic university, and so on. Having stated their needs in the way they do, the dissenting faculty raise a broad array of options (including the dean's sole option) to consider in deciding what should be done.

This case illustrates a common pitfall encountered in the definition of needs: the premature offering of a solution to the needs problem. Recognizing and articulating needs is an evolutionary process. It is important that at the outset we leave as many options open as possible. As we go through the effort of articulating needs, we obtain more and more pertinent information that allows us to narrow down the options. Only after we have gone through this process do we have enough information to consider seriously the specific solutions to satisfying needs.

Addressing the Needs of the Wrong End-Users

In the earliest stages of the needs/requirements life cycle, when we first grapple with trying to identify and formulate needs, we should find ourselves struggling to clarify *whose* needs should be addressed. If we do not raise that question, there is a good chance that we will address the needs of the wrong end-users. Two possible situations stand out here: either there are multiple end-users, and we address the needs of the wrong set of end-users; or our personal values so color our interpretation of the end-users' needs that we wind up addressing our needs rather than theirs.

Sorting Out the Needs of Multiple End-Users. Up until now, I have been talking about satisfying end-user needs as if it were clear who the end-user is. In practice, there are often multiple end-users to contend with, and their needs typically do not dovetail. In fact, their needs may actually conflict. Given these circumstances, a project planner must sort through the contending needs, determine which needs are most important, and articulate a composite need that captures their most significant features. The following case study shows that, even in a relatively simple situation, it is not easy to determine whose needs should be addressed.

     LEGAL OFFICE OF THE DEPARTMENT OF NATIONAL WELL-BEING. The legal office of the U.S. Department of National Well-Being has fifty attorneys. All office records regarding internal administrative matters are maintained manually by an administrative assistant. Office automation is limited to the use of four stand-alone word processors (although the great bulk of paperwork is still produced on standard electric typewriters rather than on word processors).

     John Roberts, the new chief counsel who has just joined the department from a major law firm, is surprised to find such low usage of new information technology. Not only are administrative matters handled manually, but staff attorneys have no access to computerized legal research data bases such as LEXIS, which are employed routinely in law firms and law schools.

     Unfortunately, Mr. Roberts shares with most attorneys anxiety and befuddlement regarding technical things and is not certain how to go about remedying the office's information processing deficiencies. Indeed, he is not even absolutely certain that a true deficiency exists.

Allen Kaye is the only attorney in the legal office with a technical background. He has recently become fascinated with personal computers and their day-to-day applications. He purchased a Micro-G computer for use at home and now wants to turn his attention to the Stellar Max personal computer, which is fast becoming the standard for the workplace. He meets with Mr. Roberts and argues forcefully that their office is living in an information stone age. He shows Mr. Roberts an article that recently appeared in the New York Times *describing the power of the Stellar Max in the workplace. He points out that this machine, if equipped with a modem, could also be used to access various legal research data bases. After half an hour of persuasive argument, he convinces Mr. Roberts to order a Stellar Max for the office.*

Several months pass before the computer arrives. Meanwhile, another legal office attorney, Robin Smith, has become intrigued with the possible uses of the computer in her work. She talks to Mr. Kaye about her desire to learn something about the Stellar Max, and Mr. Kaye, delighted to find someone who shares his interest in computer applications, eagerly enumerates the computer's possibilities. At the end of the discussion, however, he turns serious for a moment and warns Ms. Smith that she should try to contain her enthusiasm so that not too many attorneys become interested in using the computer. Should this happen, he anticipates that both he and Ms. Smith will have to fight tooth and nail for time at the machine.

Unfortunately for Ms. Smith, enthusiasm is no substitute for substantive knowledge of how computers operate. She recognizes this and decides that the most efficient way to learn about software and computer operations is through formal training. She receives permission from Mr. Roberts to approach the training office of the department to learn whether they can provide training assistance on use of the Stellar Max. The training office head responds that, although the department has capabilities to train agency personnel to use microcomputer software and hardware, it has already overcommitted its meager resources and will be unable to assist the legal office. Furthermore, he refuses to approve the use of outside contractors for training legal office personnel, because his office cannot adequately monitor the quality of such training—and because such outside training undercuts the raison d'être of his office.

Five months later, a visitor to the legal office sees Allen Kaye bent over a Stellar Max, lost to all things save his machine and his data base, word processing, and spreadsheet software. An attorney laughingly tells the visitor that Mr. Kaye is the office's computer nut, spending eight hours a day, five days a week, on the machine. He adds that no one else in the office knows the first thing about computers, so no one has the slightest idea what Kaye is doing.

Multiple Users, Multiple Needs. The preceding case illustrates how most organizations typically deal with the needs/requirements life cycle. Needs are identified and articulated in the most haphazard way. A systematic needs assessment would have shown that the overall need to automate the legal office could be broken into a number of specific needs that differ according to different end-users. If John Roberts, the chief counsel, had asked Allen Kaye to articulate the office's information needs more precisely, and if he had required Kaye to raise the questions listed earlier in this chapter during the discussion of needs articulation, he would have learned that the different constituencies in his office have their own specific information needs. Consider the following actors in the legal office, and their needs.

• *John Roberts, the chief counsel.* Roberts would like to have his office run as smoothly and efficiently as possible. To the extent that office automation increases office productivity, he sees it as good. In addition, with an automated office, he may be able to improve his access to timely information on legal and administrative activities within the office. Finally, by replacing machines that clunk with machines that hum, he may impress upper management with his grasp of modern technologies, which could help satisfy his need for career advancement.

• *Legal office attorneys.* Perhaps the strongest information need facing the attorneys (including Allen Kaye and Robin Smith) is rapid and full access to legal information. This information is crucial for them to formulate effective legal opinions. The most important aspect of office automation for them is access to the computerized legal data bases.

• *Allen Kaye.* Kaye has expressed a need to upgrade his computer skills. Perhaps this need is rooted in a desire to do the best job he can, or in satisfaction of curiosity about computer technology, or in a desire to upgrade his skills to make him more attractive in the job market.

• *Administrative assistant.* Since the administrative assistant is charged with maintaining all office records (for example, time sheets, budgets, and personnel files), her information needs focus on data creation, manipulation, and retrieval. On a more personal level, she may see automation as filling a need for greater authority and prestige, since as chief administrative staff member she would clearly play an important role in maintaining a computerized system.

• *Secretaries.* Secretarial information needs revolve around their principal clerical task: typing reports and legal opinions. These needs are addressed primarily by word processing equipment, which allows a handful of secretaries to do the work of many secretaries working only with typewriters. It should be noted, however, that satisfaction of this professional need may create problems for secretaries, since it may lead to their unemployment.

• *All actors in the legal office.* One need that all the actors in the legal office share is to receive training on the new technology. Allen Kaye is the only one in the office who uses the Stellar Max, because he is the only individual who knows how to use it. He learned to use the computer through self-instruction, and he was successful in this because he was highly motivated. Because they lack microcomputer training, the other staff members never warmed up to the Stellar Max and were never able to see how it could help them improve their productivity.

In the final analysis, the only need that was fully addressed and satisfied was Allen Kaye's need to upgrade his computer skills. The project to automate the legal office was an outstanding success from Kaye's viewpoint but a failure from the perspective of the other actors. The project could have been handled more effectively if a systematic needs analysis had been carried out. A good needs analyst would have unearthed the full array of needs that had a bearing on office automation—including professional, personal, and psychological needs.

Establishing Priorities: The Needs Hierarchy. When there are multiple end-users—and there often are—the needs recognition and articulation effort can become complex. In part, this is a function of the fact that there are more needs to deal with. It is hard enough to get a handle on a single need. It is harder still to come to grips with several needs, particularly when these needs reflect the different orientations and requirements of different end-users. The needs are not likely to dovetail perfectly. They may even conflict with each other. It is clear that priorities must be established among them. Not all needs are equal in importance, nor do they have equal costs and technical risks associated with them.

How do we reconcile the different, often conflicting, needs of the different end-users? How can we generate a set of reasonably consistent and focused needs that will serve as the basis of our project plan? The answer is to create a *needs hierarchy* during the needs articulation phase of the needs/requirements life cycle. The needs hierarchy is a diagram that shows the full range of needs that exist for a given problem, and the relationship of these needs to each other. A view of a partial needs hierarchy for the legal office case is offered in Figure 5.1. We will assume that this needs hierarchy was put together by a small team of staff workers in the legal office working closely with the chief counsel, administrative assistant, staff attorneys, and secretaries; thus, we have reasonable assurance that the hierarchy has incorporated the input of most or all of the relevant actors in the legal office. Each item in the hierarchy was included only after the team achieved a consensus that the item belonged in the hierarchy.

As Figure 5.1. shows, needs appearing at one level incorporate needs appearing at the next level down. The dominant need, shown at the highest level, is to automate the legal office. This can be achieved by improving access to legal data bases, improving the efficiency of report production, and improving maintenance of office records (see the second-highest level of Figure 5.1). Note that these needs reflect the interests of multiple end-users—the staff attorneys, office secretaries, and administrative assistant, respectively. Within the need to improve access to legal data, Figure 5.1 shows that three subsidiary needs must be addressed: the

Figure 5.1. Needs Hierarchy for Legal Office Automation Project.

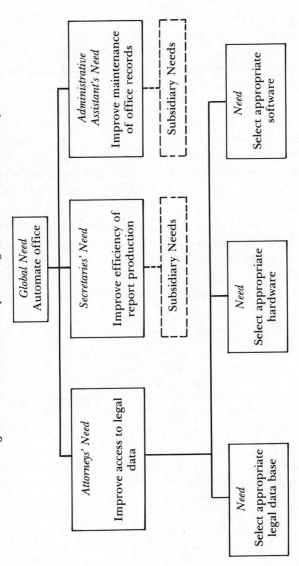

need to select an appropriate data base, to select appropriate hardware, and to select appropriate software.

At any given level of the hierarchy, decisions must be made to establish priorities among the needs found at that level. For example, in the second level of Figure 5.1, which need is most significant—to improve access to legal data, to improve the efficiency of report production, or to improve maintenance of office records? The answer to this question is determined by a needs analysis team, which takes into account many factors, including the mission of the legal office, costs, political factors, and technical feasibility. If the legal office has a superabundance of resources and it seems operationally possible to satisfy all three needs, the team may feel that all three needs can be tackled simultaneously. If, on the other hand, the needs analysis team feels that the legal office has the ability to handle only one need at a time, it will recommend that the highest-ranked need be addressed first.

Figure 5.2. Overall Needs Hierarchy for Legal Office.

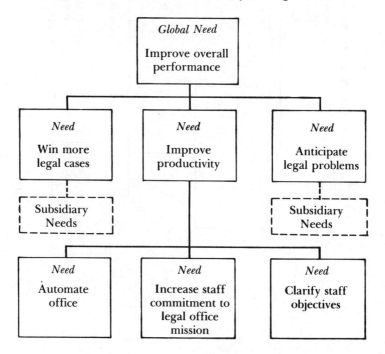

It should be noted that the needs hierarchy can be extended to higher (and lower) levels of aggregation than portrayed in Figure 5.1. In Figure 5.2, we see that the need to automate the legal office was subsidiary to a need to improve the office's productivity, which in turn was subsidiary to the office's highest need, to improve overall office performance. The elaborateness and detail of a needs hierarchy should be determined by the context of the situation being faced. A team charged with articulating needs for an office automation project would not be interested in the macropurview of Figure 5.2. A needs hierarchy as pictured in Figure 5.1 would be most relevant to them.

I have only hinted here at how the needs of multiple end-users can be handled. The needs hierarchy is a useful tool for this purpose. Constructing a needs hierarchy forces us to act systematically to identify relevant actors and their needs. It also requires us to make explicit choices as to what is most important to us. Finally, use of a well-chosen needs analysis team to develop the needs hierarchy through a consensus-building process increases the likelihood that the articulated needs reflect the true needs of end-users.

Distorting the End-User's Needs. There is always a danger that the individuals analyzing the needs of the end-user will alter the statement of those needs so that they more closely reflect their own biases than the end-user's true needs. Sometimes this alteration is undertaken consciously, but I suspect that usually it is not. If you were to point out to needs analysts that their articulation of the end-users' needs was strongly distorted by their own values and perceptions, they would probably be surprised.

There are a number of ways that end-user needs are distorted in this fashion. Three common ways are gold-plating of needs, selective filtering of end-user needs, and practicing the father-knows-best approach to needs recognition and articulation.

• *Gold-plating of needs.* We live in an era where new technology is glorified and obsolescence is abhorred. Purchasing agents in organizations are extremely sensitive to the issue of obsolescence. One of their big questions is "Will the hardware

I buy today be obsolete one or two years from now?'' Since this is often a difficult question to answer, the safest course of action may be to buy the most advanced hardware available.

This orientation carries over to defining needs. An end-user may have a need to get from A to B in a certain period of time. This need may be perfectly well served by providing the end-user with a 1970 Ford. However, the needs analyst, who is aware of state-of-the-art automobile systems, may upgrade the end-user's needs to include a need for climate control within the vehicle, quadraphonic sound, cruise control, and so on. While the end-user may need only a Ford, she may get a Cadillac—in order to satisfy the needs analyst's enhancements of her needs. The problem here is largely one of waste, of underutilized capacity. But at least the end-user can use the Cadillac to get from A to B. Things could be worse. Consider the case of a needs analyst who is an extreme technology enthusiast. He may articulate the end-user's simple need in such a manner that the only way to satisfy this need is to order a state-of-the-art F-15 fighter, which will get the end-user from A to B very quickly indeed! In this case, of course, the problem is that the system as defined by the needs analyst does not satisfy the end-user's needs at all; consequently, the system emerging from the gold-plated needs will not be used.

The problem of gold-plating needs is fairly common in organizations that do not face serious resource constraints. The military services are a prime example. New projects are often conceived as initially simple and relatively cost-effective, but needs may be redefined so that they take into account every conceivable contingency a weapons system might encounter. By the end of one or two years, the original, simple conception metamorphoses into something extremely complex—and expensive. Lean and hungry organizations do not engage in much gold-plating of needs, not because they are inherently less inclined to obtain the most advanced technology but because the discipline of the small bank account forces them to take a more parsimonious view of their needs.

• *Selective filtering of end-user needs.* There is an old saying that has important implications for the analysis of end-user needs: "To a four-year-old boy with a hammer, all the world is a nail." We can just as well say that to an accountant, all the world is a spreadsheet; or to a scientist, all the world is a set of mathematically describable physical relationships; or to a politician, all the world is potential voters. Each of us sees the world through a filter that has been developed over a lifetime and reflects our experiences, values, and training.

Our filters clearly color how we perceive things. A difficulty arises when our perceptions deviate dramatically from reality. In such a situation, our response to problems may bear little relationship to what is needed to solve them. In the context of articulating needs, we may find an end-user telling a needs analyst, "I need a better way to keep track of the services my clinic offers to clients." What a computer-oriented needs analyst may hear is "I need a computerized, client-directed management information system." Consequently, what is ultimately delivered to the end-user may be an elaborate and expensive computer system, when his needs could have been adequately satisfied with a stack of three-by-five-inch index cards. Once again the consequence of distorting end-user needs may be the underutilization, misutilization, or nonutilization of a project's deliverables.

The best way to bypass this problem is to have the needs recognition and articulation tasks carried out by a *group* of people, each having a different background and each being capable of viewing end-user needs from a different perspective. Of course, close contact with the end-user is also important.

• *Practicing the father-knows-best approach to needs recognition and articulation.* I know a man who in the mid-1960s served in the Peace Corps in an Andean village. One of his goals was to carry out a small demonstration project to show the local Indians how to raise healthy, plump hogs by using modern animal husbandry. At the end of several months, the two objects of his attention—Napoleon and Josephine—were the finest-looking hogs in the region, a tribute to modern agricultural science and the Peace Corps worker's diligence. The Indians admired the outcome of this demonstration project, yet none of them adopted the methods employed by my acquaintance. He asked several of them, "Don't you want to raise nice hogs like Napoleon and Josephine?" and they responded, "Certainly, we do."

"Well, why don't you employ the hog-raising techniques I showed you in my demonstration project?" he persisted.

They responded, "We don't employ these techniques because we figure that in your approach it costs more to raise the hogs than we can recover by selling them. Right now, it costs us nothing to raise hogs, because we give them scraps and let them eat whatever they can find in the streets and fields. Whatever price we get for them in the market is almost all profit to us. So our hogs are small, but at least they're profitable."

This story illustrates something that often happens during the needs articulation phase, something I call the father-knows-best syndrome. Usually the people working on the needs articulation task have been selected to carry out this task because they have the experience and technical competence to translate the end-user's often vague perception of a need into something concrete and workable. In these circumstances, it is easy for the needs articulators to assume a paternalistic posture and to feel that they know what is best for the end-user, even when the end-user shows resistance to their suggestions. Because they are experts, they often *do* know what is best for the end-user. However, if they encounter user resistance to their approach and choose to ignore the user's deeply felt concerns (when these concerns are silly and uneducated), the project emerging from the needs they articulate is likely to produce a deliverable that will be underutilized, misutilized, or not utilized at all by the end-user. Sometimes, of course, the experts do *not* know what is best for the end-user, as was the case in our hog-raising example. In any event, individuals involved in articulating needs should avoid taking a paternalistic approach to their work, since there is nothing to be gained from it, and much to be lost.

Conclusion

I have devoted a whole chapter to the issue of recognizing and articulating end-user needs because projects arise in order to address needs. As I said at the outset of this chapter, needs are the driving force behind projects. If we do a bad job of articulating needs, our project will have been built on a foundation of sand. Major problems *will* arise in the project. Articulating needs is serious business but receives little attention in either the theory or the practice of project management.

It is interesting to note that little or no attention is directed toward end-user needs in the conventional project management literature. For example, one of the most comprehensive conventional project management works, *Project Management Handbook* (Cleland and King, 1983), a very good book, completely overlooks the issue of end-user needs. We encounter a different situation in the information system development literature. Here inadequate recognition and articulation of user needs is seen to be a major cause of project failure, and a substantial literature has developed to deal with the issue of satisfying end-user needs. Markus's *Systems in Organizations: Bugs and Features*, for example, provides a thorough and insightful treatment of what happens when end-user needs are not met or are only partially addressed.

In regard to the *practice* of project management, my personal experience suggests an overall disregard for the issues covered in this chapter. Not surprisingly, there does not seem to be much goodwill between end-users and project staff. When the two sides persist in miscommunicating and frustration levels get high, users often harbor the view that project staff are unresponsive and suffer technical tunnel vision, while project staff see users as fickle, aimless, unknowledgeable, and naive.

The pity is that so many project problems are rooted in poor needs recognition and articulation. Should these matters receive sufficient attention at the outset of the project, many of these problems would not arise.

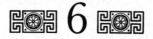

6

Specifying What the Project Should Accomplish

For most of us, being misunderstood is a common occurrence, something that happens on a daily basis. At the restaurant the waiter brings us our dinner and we note that the baked potato is filled with sour cream, even though we expressly requested *no* sour cream. For Mother's Day we order a dozen roses to be sent to our mother and we are aghast to receive a call from her thanking us so much for the lovely carnations. Our mail-order drapes arrive—eight inches shorter than we ordered.

Projects are filled with similar misunderstandings between end-users and project staff. What end-users order—or, more accurately, what they *think* they order—is often not what they get. Consider the following conversation between an office worker and a painter contracted to paint his office.

Office worker: Not only did you paint my office walls blue, but you painted the ceiling blue as well.

Painter: You asked me to paint the room blue, and now you've got a blue room.

Office worker: But the blue ceiling is oppressive. Ceilings should never be the same color as the walls. They should always be a lighter color.

Painter: You asked for a blue room. You're lucky I didn't paint the floor blue as well.

This conversation captures in a nutshell the essence of a major source of misunderstandings on projects: the inadequate statement of end-user requirements. The office worker's description of how he wanted the room painted meant one thing to him and another to the painter. As a consequence, the room was not painted to the office worker's satisfaction. Had his requirements been more carefully stipulated, he probably would have had what he wanted.

The blame for the poor specification of requirements does not rest entirely on his shoulders. The painter must share some culpability. It was clearly in her interest to make sure she understood exactly what the office worker wanted. As a professional painter, she should devise an approach to dealing with clients that allows her to determine precisely what their requirements are. For example, before beginning each paint job, she might give the client a checklist, asking what colors the walls should be, the ceilings, the trim. Otherwise, clients will continue to be unhappy when she does not do what they want, and they will see to it that she is unhappy as well.

One major objective of those who are effective in designing and implementing projects is to reduce such misunderstandings to a minimum. This can be done with the careful specification of end-user requirements.

The Nature of Requirements

As we saw in the last chapter, requirements specify what the project deliverable should look like. They can be divided into two basic categories. *Functional requirements* describe the characteristics of the deliverable in ordinary, nontechnical language. They should be understandable to the end-user, and the end-user should play a major, direct role in their development. *Technical requirements* describe the features of the deliverable (for example, its physical dimensions and performance specifications) in detailed technical terms. These technical specifications offer project staff crucial guidance on what they should be doing on the project. Because of their technical nature, technical requirements are unlikely to be understood by the end-user. In this chapter, most of our attention will focus on functional requirements.

Project requirements are important for at least two reasons. First, they are a tangible embodiment of the user's needs. Needs emerge, are recognized and carefully articulated, and then are translated into requirements, which serve as the basis of the project plan. In the final analysis, project planning reduces to the effort of determining how best to meet requirements. If they are misspecified or poorly specified, the plan will be inadequate.

Second, requirements are important because they define the project team's obligations to the end-user. Carefully specified project requirements detail the team's responsibilities. On projects run under contract, the specified requirements are written as a statement of work (SOW), and compliance or noncompliance with the contract is determined by resolving whether the contractor has fulfilled the SOW.

Problems with Requirements

Requirements-related problems are one of the principal sources of cost and schedule overruns. They may lead to rejection of the deliverable or to major reworking of project tasks. Furthermore, they contribute substantially to what I perceive to be the most serious category of project failure: the production of a deliverable that is never used or is misused. Requirements-related problems result in several ways: the requirements that are specified are incorrect; the requirements are imprecise and ambiguous; the requirements shift as the project is carried out.

Regardless of the specific nature of the requirements-related problem, its consequences unfold with consistent regularity. Here is what happens: During the course of the project, the end-user becomes aware that what the project staff are developing is not what he or she wants. This may reflect the fact that the project staff are working on something completely at variance with what he or she wants (incorrect requirements); or they have misinterpreted his or her stated desires (imprecise, ambiguous requirements); or the end-user has changed his or her mind about what the project staff should develop (shifting requirements). At any rate, the end-user and the project staff are out of sync, and the flow of the project is interrupted.

If the project staff respond to the end-user's concerns and do what the end-user wants—and they really should if they have grossly misconstrued the desires of the end-user—the project will have to be replanned, delays will occur, and cost overruns are likely. If they do not act in accordance with the end-user's desires, the project's deliverable is not likely to be very meaningful to the end-user, suggesting that the project was a waste of time and resources.

Project managers are faced with a no-win situation here. When requirements-related problems arise, project managers encounter either the likely prospect of cost and schedule overruns or strong end-user dissatisfaction. Their best bet is to avoid this problem before it surfaces; once it arises, there will be serious trouble. The problem can largely be avoided if they take great pains to undertake the articulation of end-user needs carefully, and then work closely with end-users in writing unambiguous functional requirements. They should also recognize that end-users are often fickle characters and should take precautions to avoid being taken by surprise by sudden end-user shifts in requirements.

These guidelines are only general prescriptions for success. To make them workable, we examine the three principal areas of requirements-related problems in detail.

Incorrect Requirements

We saw in the last chapter that there are many ways in which end-user needs can be misconstrued and misrepresented. For example, the needs addressed may be those of the wrong end-user, the articulated needs may reflect the biases of the needs articulator, and inherently fuzzy needs may be misinterpreted. In any such cases, functional requirements built upon poorly articulated needs will be off the mark. This is a certainty! The final deliverable (assuming the project gets that far) will bear little or no relationship to what the end-user wants.

The best way to avoid positing incorrect requirements is to make sure that end-user needs have been properly articulated. A large share of Chapter Five was dedicated to suggesting ways to carry out the needs recognition and articulation tasks effectively, so it is not necessary to rehash the earlier material here, except to offer a summary of steps that should be taken.

First, project planners should recognize the inherent difficulty of articulating needs. Needs tend to be fuzzy; even those holding them generally aren't quite sure what the needs are. Recognition of the difficulty in articulating needs is important, because it encourages the individuals charged with articulation to give this matter the attention it deserves. Too often these individuals rush in with packaged solutions to problems they don't really understand.

Second, project planners should identify who the most relevant end-users are. In most situations, project planners will be dealing with multiple end-users, only some of whose needs should be addressed in the project. They should avoid organizing their projects around the needs of peripheral or nonrelevant end-users.

Third, project planners should work closely with end-users in articulating their needs. Needs articulation entails a certain amount of hand holding; the needs articulator and the end-user should work closely together to hammer out a well-formulated and accurate statement of what it is the end-user needs.

Fourth, project planners should be aware of the most common pitfalls associated with needs articulation. They should avoid gold-plating needs (that is, offering end-users more than they need), imposing their own needs on end-users, and assuming a paternalistic, father-knows-best attitude in dealing with end-users.

Imprecise and Ambiguous Requirements

One extremely common problem arises when requirements are posited in such a way that they are imprecise and ambiguous, subject to different interpretations regarding their meaning. Imprecise requirements are invitations to problems. When requirements are ambiguously specified, two people can look at the exact same statement and disagree on what it means. The disagreement can become vehement, since it is clear to each party what the specification is saying, and the fact that the other party does not view the specification "correctly" is attributed to obstinacy, stupidity, or outright dishonesty.

There are various reasons why requirements are specified imprecisely. Some of these reasons are legitimate and understandable. Others reflect sloppy thinking, impatience, or a conscious desire to obfuscate things. Following is a listing of the more obvious reasons for the imprecise specification of requirements.

The Nature of Human Language. Human language is naturally ambiguous. While this ambiguity makes for interesting poetry, it is not well suited to describing the requirements of project deliverables. For example, we may specify that we want to furnish our waiting room with chairs that are fire engine red. This immediately conjures up an image in most of our minds of a bright red color. But there are many varieties of bright red. (Of course, we could go to our local fire department to get a better idea of what fire engine red is, but this would not be very useful in my neighborhood, where the fire trucks are yellow.) We can be more precise in specifying our color if we specifically request a particular upholstery fabric with a given color identification number, or if we attach to the requirements statement a sample of the desired color. If we want to carry this matter of precision even further, we can describe the color according to its wavelength in the visible light spectrum.

This discussion points out the difficulty of depending on human language to describe requirements. For requirements to be precise, we must often supplement our verbal descriptions with additional supporting material—drawings, samples, maps, photographs, technical data. We can reduce the imprecision in the verbal portion of the requirements statement by describing what we want in excruciating detail, leaving nothing to the imagination. In this last instance, however, we run the risk of overwhelming project staff with impenetrable verbiage that they may choose to ignore.

Deliberate Imprecision for Flexibility. Sometimes requirements are stated ambiguously on purpose, simply to maintain flexibility in the project. This approach is common in state-of-the-art projects, on which there is generally great uncertainty about how the project will proceed. The fear is that the precise statement of requirements will constrict project staff in their work, discouraging them from exploiting unanticipated opportunities as they arise. Deliberate imprecision is also common in projects that are filled with conditional outcomes. These are projects on which in response to the question "What is it that you want?" the end-user responds, "It depends on how things work out." The danger with this approach is that the project may drift aimlessly. As a consequence, it runs the risk of never being concluded, or of producing a deliverable that meets no one's needs. This is precisely the outcome of many basic research projects.

Human Conflict Preventing Consensus. When people cannot achieve a consensus on what it is that should emerge from a project, they may be unable to generate clear-cut requirements. They may postpone hard choices until later, hoping that the conflict among them will be resolved and things will somehow straighten themselves out. What is likely to happen, of course, is that the loosely phrased requirements will take on a life of their own and lead to a deliverable that satisfies none of the contending parties. Given the tendency of poorly formulated requirements to cause project troubles, it is usually better to make the hard choices as early as possible in the project life cycle. These choices will have to be reckoned with some day; if they are addressed later in the project, and it is determined that the project has been moving in the wrong direction, the consequences for the budget and schedule may be devastating.

Inherently Nebulous Information-Age Projects. Information-age projects often deal with intangibles or "semitangibles," whereas traditional projects in the construction and engineering areas deal with things you can touch and readily see. For example, in designing a project to carry out a marketing study, we are dealing primarily with abstractions—consumers, consumer preferences, hypothetical product prices, potential competitors, mythical competing products, and so forth. Trying to get a firm grip on these abstractions is something like trying to grab a handful of sand.

Seasoned professionals who spend their lives working with intangibles develop the capacity to "see" what the end product will look like, just as a draftsperson can look at a blank sheet of paper and "see" the drawing that will ultimately emerge. The problem is that end-users are generally not seasoned professionals accustomed, say, to designing on-line information systems or undertaking sophisticated marketing studies. In trying to visualize the deliverable, they cannot see anything but an amorphous blob. Only as the project evolves and takes shape do they begin to have an inkling of what is being developed. Now that they can see what is emerging, they may not like it and may demand that the project take a different turn to produce something that is more to their liking. This is a very common occurrence with projects dealing with intangibles and semitangibles.

What project staff must do to minimize problems created by the inherently ethereal nature of their projects is to help end-users "see" the results of the project as early as possible. They should make frequent use of visual tools, such as drawings, flow diagrams, and tables, and they can do what architects and engineers regularly do in their projects: create simple prototypes of the deliverable, which they can show to the end-user. Rather than build a physical model of a building or an airplane, they would put together simple back-of-the-envelope mockups of the thing they are developing—a scaled-down computerized accounting system, or a sample market study, for example. A methodology has recently been created to help project planners and managers use prototypes effectively in information projects. It is called *application prototyping*, and I will discuss it in more detail later in this chapter.

End-Users' Lack of Expertise. Everybody knows that an expert is someone who is very good at doing something. A tennis expert is good at playing tennis, a computer expert is good at writing code, a legal expert is good at interpreting the law, and so forth. By the same token, someone who is not an expert will find it difficult to do these things well. End-users are generally not experts with regard to the technical content of the projects carried out to meet their needs. They may have expertise in other areas, but this other expertise may be only marginally helpful to them in formulating needs and requirements for their project. Albert Einstein, for example, was a brilliant theoretical physicist of international renown. To my generation—children during Einstein's last years—his name is virtually synonymous with the word *genius*. Yet I doubt if Dr. Einstein would have been very effective in describing the precise requirements of an accounting system to assist Princeton's Institute for Advanced Studies (his employer) in keeping better track of how he and his colleagues spent their research funds.

One important task of the project team is to educate end-users about relevant features of the potential deliverable. Certainly, end-users cannot be expected to know everything, but just how well educated should they be? This is a difficult question to answer specifically. There are dangers with both over-education and undereducation. If too much effort is devoted to educating end-users, they may be overwhelmed with detail that they cannot—and possibly don't want to—understand. In this case, the well-meaning attempt at end-user education may produce an effect that is completely opposite to what was intended. Feeling themselves lost in a miasma of incomprehensible technicalities, end-users may withdraw from the needs articulation and requirements specification efforts and leave the project definition in the hands of the experts. These experts, unfortunately, often have little understanding of what the end-users will ultimately find acceptable.

On the other hand, if little or no effort is devoted to educating end-users, they will not know enough to be useful partners in the needs articulation and requirements specification efforts. Their input into the project definition process will be ill-informed and may steer the project into fruitless side excursions. Ultimately, a deliverable will be produced that will not be very useful to them.

Project staff should be sensitive to the issue of end-user education. The temptation is to ignore this education altogether—

and possibly even to intimidate the end-user with expertise. Let's face it: end-users can be a big pain. They don't know what they want or what is good for them, yet this doesn't stop them from telling project staff how to do their job. When end-users timidly offer suggestions, experts who really don't want end-user kibitzing often react by overwhelming them with terms and statistics beyond their ken, hoping to intimidate them with a technical whirlwind. Perhaps this tactic gains some momentary peace for the project staff, but in the long run it may lead to the creation of deliverables that end-users do not want.

How much should end-users know? In general, end-users should know enough to be able to contribute meaningful input to the needs articulation and requirements specification efforts. They should also know enough so that they are not surprised with the final outcome. The specific amount of education that should be directed at them has to be determined on a case-by-case basis.

Oversights on the Part of Project Planners. The final reason I shall offer on why requirements are stated imprecisely is more pedestrian than the others. Simply put, requirements may be stated imprecisely because of sheer oversight, reflecting an incomplete understanding of what the project should entail and what the deliverable should be. In asking the painter in our earlier example to paint our office pale blue, we may exclude the requirement to keep the ceiling white because it does not occur to us that this is an issue.

These kinds of oversights occur on all but the most routine projects. There is a certain inevitability to them. They occur because we are not omniscient and because we lack sufficient imagination to identify every possible meaningful contingency that our project should address. One way to minimize such oversights is to go to those who will actually carry out the assigned tasks and ask them what kinds of contingencies might arise that should be dealt with in the project specifications. A good long-run approach for dealing with such oversights is to compile a project-by-project checklist of requirements that should be addressed on projects carried out in the organization. As more and more project experience is gained, the list will grow both in depth and breadth. Workers in the construction industry are familiar with this kind of list.

Shifting Requirements

The third and final broad area of requirements-related problems focuses on those problems associated with shifting requirements. Projects are dynamic things; so it should not come as a surprise that, as a project evolves, there are strong pressures to modify the original requirements. However, modification may play havoc with the project plan, which is built upon specified requirements, and may lead to cost and schedule overruns. Four common situations resulting in changes in requirements are illustrated in the following cases.

BUYER'S REMORSE. *Dr. Maureen Shea is administrator of Marvin Gelb Memorial Hospital. This hospital is overcrowded, with three patients typically occupying a single room. Dr. Shea and her staff have long entertained a dream of building a new wing onto the hospital, which would dramatically ameliorate the crowded condition. When a three-point plunge in mortgage rates occurs, Dr. Shea seizes the opportunity and enters into a contract with a construction firm to build the new wing. The new wing will accommodate 120 beds, a major addition to the patient-handling capability of the hospital.*

No sooner is the contract with the builder signed than Dr. Shea reads in the local paper a series of articles on the growing popularity of inexpensive outpatient care facilities in the region. She begins to worry that perhaps she has bitten off more than she can chew with her expansion of the hospital. Five months into the project, after a foundation has been poured and the skeleton of the new wing has risen from the ground, Dr. Shea begins discussions with the builder to revise the construction plans so that the facility will accommodate only 60 new beds instead of the original 120. She is shocked to learn that this 50 percent reduction in the wing's capacity will save only 15 percent in construction charges.

This case illustrates a phenomenon that real estate agents and car dealers are familiar with. It is so common in these lines of business that it has been given a name: buyer's remorse. It is also common in project management, especially with controversial or high-risk projects. After much thought and debate, a decision is made to launch a costly project, and no sooner is the decision made than those responsible for it have second thoughts. They may now try to scale down—or even eliminate—the project, in order to reduce some of the deleterious consequences they imagine will hit them if the project does not work out as expected. This scaling down may be very expensive, especially if the project is well under way, since it entails major changes in the original project plan. When this situation arises, the project manager must make it clear to the end-user that changes to the plan will be expensive.

INSURMOUNTABLE OBSTACLES. Marsha Bronfman is a graduate student working on her doctoral dissertation. Her dissertation project focuses on the public health problems of a developing country. Central to her study is a questionnaire survey of public health practitioners in the country. The questionnaire is designed to identify major obstacles to establishing an effective public health program in the country. She spends two months developing and testing the questionnaire. When it is ready, she sends out 350 copies to the principal public health workers in the country. A few days after mailing out the questionnaire, she receives a visit from an official of the ministry of health, telling her that she had no authority to conduct the survey and that she is forbidden to do further work on it. Ms. Bronfman suddenly finds herself persona non grata in the country. What is worse, from her perspective, her doctoral dissertation is jeopardized, since it was designed to focus on the results of the survey analysis. If she is going to complete her dissertation, she will have to revise her research strategy completely.

The sudden appearance of insurmountable obstacles, such as those encountered by Ms. Bronfman, is a common experience on projects. Any project that blazes new trails runs a strong risk of encountering such obstacles. With technical projects, for example, we are almost assured that technical glitches will force us to utter that age-old expostulation, ''Well, I guess it's back to the drawing board!''

FLIGHTS OF FANCY. Brian Davis and his design team are developing a new toaster for Appliance Masters Co. They spend two weeks working closely with Daniel Seligman, vice-president of new product development with the appliance firm. Mr. Seligman is a highly creative individual—the classic idea man—and he offers several novel suggestions for features that should be built into the new toaster. Davis accepts the suggestions and begins building a prototype of the new toaster.

Two months later, Seligman visits the design shop to see how the toaster is progressing. While viewing the nearly finished prototype, he becomes quite excited. "I've just had a brainstorm," he exlaims. "Let's include a voice synthesizer chip in the toaster, enabling the toaster to 'talk' to the user." The design team members, recognizing that this suggestion would require a major redesign of the product, look at Brian Davis with apprehension. "We'll do it," says Davis, and the design team members groan inwardly.

Three months later, Seligman returns to the design shop to review the nearly completed prototype of the talking toaster. The demonstration he sees causes him to jump with glee. "This is great," he says. "This is the stuff of science fiction! You know, we should carry the toaster one step further than we have. What we produce should not be a mere toaster; it should be an information center, the brains for all kitchen appliances. Look into this, will you, Brian?" Brian nods his head in agreement while performing some lightning calculations in his head. The latest request will extend the project by at least nine months and will require doubling the design team staff.

Seligman's vision of the toaster's possibilities evolved with the physical development of the toaster itself. As the new toaster took on tangible shape, Seligman's imagination was stimulated to come up with new possibilities for the toaster. Such a phenomenon is common on projects. While suggested changes in the project requirements may ultimately lead to a superior product, they can create serious problems for the project manager. Changes in the requirements are not cost-free. Because of such changes, schedules may be stretched out, costs may escalate, and other projects in the queue may have to be postponed or canceled. If changes are constantly being required, the project also runs the serious risk of never being completed.

SEIZING OPPORTUNITIES. Nancy and David Rama buy a run-down old house with a view to refurbishing it and renting it out. They hire a contractor to carry out cosmetic improvements to the house in order to make it presentable. Because the house is structurally sound, the contractor's efforts are largely dedicated to stripping off old paint, removing wallpaper, plastering cracks in walls and ceilings, repainting, and refinishing the hardwood floors. While removing paint from the mantel of the living room fireplace, the contractor discovers that the wood under the paint is a beautiful, hand-carved chestnut piece. Similarly, he finds that the banister leading down the stairs is hand-carved chestnut. As more paint is removed from window frames, it becomes clear that the Ramas have bought a quality house. Consequently, they change their original plans and decide to undertake a major renovation of the house, which will entail far more cost and effort than initially planned. They figure that the $15,000 that the major renovation will cost will enhance the value of the house by $30,000, so the added expenditure seems worthwhile.

This case is similar in many respects to the previous one; Seligman, too, no doubt saw himself as seizing opportunities that presented themselves to him. The line separating flights of fancy from seized opportunities can be a thin one. There is an important difference between the two, however. Flights of fancy typically entail an undisciplined impulse to change requirements without regard for cost, schedule, or resources. Habitual practitioners of this ''method'' of project development substitute their ad hoc approach for sound project planning. In effect, they are proponents of a plan-as-you-go school of project management. The impact of this approach on project budgets and schedules can be devastating.

Seizing opportunities, in contrast, involves a measured response to dealing with unanticipated project developments. It entails capitalizing on the unexpected. For this to be successful, it must be determined that the benefits of changing requirements outweigh costs.

Each of these four cases illustrates how easy and natural it is for requirements to change. Sometimes change is for the better and will result in improved project output. At other times change is merely disruptive and results in delays and unwise increases in costs. Project staff can count on changes in the specification of requirements, and they must learn to identify such changes as they occur. This is not always easy. Changes in requirements can be subtle and can occur very gradually, almost imperceptibly. Once professional staff have identified possible changes, they must learn to anticipate the consequences of these changes. If the consequences are strongly negative, they must alert the end-user to this fact, particularly if the end-user is the cause of the disruptive change. Without a conscious methodology for dealing with changes in the specification of requirements, project staff will be only marginally in control of their project.

The Fundamental Trade-Off in Specifying Requirements

There is a frustrating built-in conflict facing individuals charged with specifying requirements for a project. On the one hand, they might be wise to specify everything in detail. Their motto might be "Leave nothing to chance." Not only might they describe the requirements in great detail, but they could give an item-by-item directive on how the requirements should be achieved. When project managers focus on minutiae and provide detailed instructions on all the steps that have to be carried out to meet specified requirements, there is little likelihood that project staff will interpret requirements incorrectly as they undertake the project. In addition, the painstaking enumeration of detail will protect the project performers from potential accusations by the end-user that they did not do what they said they were going to do.

On the other hand, project planners might be wise to keep things as flexible as possible, so that the project can readily respond to changes in the environment that may require changes in requirements. This second, more flexible approach is based on the premise that circumstances are bound to arise that will cause alterations in the specifications of requirements.

Problems with Overspecification of Requirements

Each of the two approaches outlined above has problems associated with it. Let us begin by addressing problems with the first approach.

Insufficient Information. It is unlikely that individuals specifying requirements will have enough information to plan everything in detail; they are not omniscient. Detailed specification of requirements puts a tremendous burden on requirements analysts. Remember, they do their work *before the deliverable is produced.* If they really don't want to leave *anything* to chance, they need detailed knowledge of all the contingencies that may arise during the course of project implementation, so that they can specify different courses of action to be undertaken for these different contingencies. In practice, however, individuals writing project requirements are far from omniscient. Even the most carefully specified requirements will be based on guesswork. To the extent that these guesses are off the mark, the specified requirements may or may not be viable or relevant to the needs of the end-user.

Initiative Discouraged. Too much detail by the planners tends to discourage initiative on the part of project staff. When all the details of the requirements are spelled out for them, staff charged with implementing the plan are being told, in effect, not to take any initiative on the project: "We know best what it is you should be producing, so please don't deviate from the specs." This approach carries with it at least two possible negative consequences. One is that creativity of project staff will be discouraged. Even if staff see a way to enhance the deliverable, or if by a change of procedures they can effect time and cost savings, they are discouraged from conveying their insights to their bosses. It is unlikely that truly creative workers would be attracted to such projects.

A second possible negative consequence is that, if following the specs becomes the most significant guiding principle of a project, staff will be discouraged from assuming responsibility for doing the best job they can. Responsibility is narrowed to a simple directive: meet the specs. If project staff see a fundamental flaw in the specs, they can say, "That's not our problem. We've been told to meet the specs without questioning them, and meet them we will."

Requirements Ignored. Excessive detail in specified requirements often results in project staff ignoring them. A leave-nothing-to-chance philosophy may ultimately backfire on the requirements analyst, creating exactly the opposite effect from what was intended. Too much detail may overwhelm those charged with implementing the project. If much of the detailed material deals with relatively obvious points, there is a temptation on the part of project staff to skim over the minutiae. If the mass of detail is too difficult to digest, project staff may prefer to work things out on their own. Anyone who has tried to put together a model airplane from a kit knows what I am talking about. At the outset, you have every intention of following the instructions carefully, but after five minutes of reading very obvious material ("Before assembling the airplane, you should make sure that the parts you have match the parts listed in Exhibit A"), you decide to skip over the simple stuff. You begin painting parts and gluing them together, using the picture on the box as a guide. Occasionally you look at the assembly diagrams, but you are bewildered by the array of code letters, lines, and curves; besides, many of the parts shown in the diagrams don't look like anything you have in your kit. In the end, you have a finished product that looks reasonably similar to the airplane pictured on the box, but there are three or four remaining parts lying on the table that you never incorporated into the model airplane.

Costly Rework Efforts. Excessive rigidity in the specification of requirements may lead to costly rework efforts. Change will occur on projects. Perhaps user needs shift, or new technological developments make the deliverable obsolete in its present form, or a new labor contract escalates the salaries of project staff higher than anticipated. The details will differ from project to project, but the fact remains that *change will occur*, and this change will require us to rethink our requirements. If requirements are rigid, and deviations from them are prohibited, chances are that at some point our refusal to accommodate change will catch up with us. For example, it may become clear early in the project life cycle that meeting a particular requirement is technically unfeasible. However, owing to the rigidity of our approach to requirements, we may proceed as if there were no problem. Ultimately, we come face to face with the fact that the spec is unachievable in its present form. We have no choice but to change our requirements and redo the work we have completed. At this point, the rework effort will be quite expensive. We could have saved considerable time and money had we altered the specified requirements earlier in the project, when we first perceived the problem.

Problems with Excessive Flexibility in Specifying Requirements

Excessive flexibility in specifying requirements also has problems associated with it. Problems include:

Patchwork Deliverables. Excessive flexibility will lead to a patchwork deliverable. The specify-as-you-go approach to defining requirements can easily yield a deliverable that lacks cohesiveness. With such an approach, the deliverable reflects many ad hoc decisions rather than a comprehensive vision. To paraphrase a well-known epigram, a camel is a horse designed as a result of the ad hoc specification of requirements.

Chaotic Project Planning. Excessive flexibility will result in chaotic project planning. As we shall see in the next chapter, planning is the process of identifying how we can achieve our requirements, given the constraints of limited time and resources. If our requirements are ill-defined and evolve willy-nilly over the life of the project, our planning efforts will be chaotic. We will have no cohesive plan; rather, we will have many different plans that change in character as changes are made in the requirements.

Time and Cost Overruns. Excessive flexibility will increase the likelihood of time and cost overruns. The previous two problems associated with excessive flexibility are likely to result in time and cost overruns. A patchwork deliverable that does not meet end-user needs, for example, may result in rejection of the deliverable by the end-user and may give rise to demands to re-do the project. Clearly, if the project entails rework efforts, we will encounter both time and budget slippages.

If excessive flexibility causes chaotic planning, this will lead to major inefficiencies in the implementation of the project. We will face false starts and about-faces. Resource utilization will be haphazard, since we will never be quite sure what resources—and how many—we should be using at any given time. With such inefficiencies, it is unlikely that we will meet our original budget and schedule targets.

We see, then, that the two extremes for specifying requirements will probably yield serious problems for project staff. In specifying requirements, therefore, we should seek some middle ground—an approach that avoids the rigidity of immoderately detailed, inflexible requirements, on the one hand, and the chaos of excessively free-form requirements, on the other. To put this in a more positive light, what we want are requirements that are firm and clear enough to avoid problems of ambiguity and volatility and at the same time are sufficiently flexible to accommodate changes that are bound to occur during the course of a project.

General Guidelines for Specifying Requirements

I don't think I can overstate the observation that, along with inadequately articulated end-user needs, poorly formulated requirements stand out as an enormously significant source of grief on projects. If the requirements are stipulated incorrectly, or if they are subject to multiple interpretations, or if they are too complicated, or if they are forever changing, the whole project suffers. The good news is that many of the problems associated with requirements specification can be minimized if those involved with projects—project staff and end-users alike—pay attention to some basic guidelines.

Rule 1: State the requirement explicitly and have project staff and end-users sign off on it. Too often, especially on small, informal projects, requirements are *implied* rather than *stated explicitly.* For example, George says to Martha, ''Write up a proposal to bid on that Molsen job, will you?'' Martha agrees, and four days later she turns in a document that George finds to be too short, lacking in methodological rigor, and emphasizing the wrong issues. George calls Martha in and chews her out. ''This isn't what I asked for,'' he chides, pointing out its various shortcomings to Martha in detail.

Two features of this incident stand out. First, it is ludicrous for George to say, ''This isn't what I asked for,'' since he never really did say what it was that he wanted. *Of course* what Martha delivered was not what George asked for. This was assured by the fact that George never conveyed anything but the vaguest sense of his requirements. A second interesting feature is this: Only after the project has failed from George's perspective does he sit down and elucidate what he expects out of the Molsen proposal. That is, in pointing out the problems with the proposal, he is hinting at what his requirements are ex post facto. Even here he is *implying* his requirements rather than stating them explicitly and systematically.

In general, it is a good idea to be explicit in stating requirements. The explicit listing of requirements serves as a contract, focusing on what it is that a user wants and what project staff have agreed to deliver. As with any contract linking user and producer, it is wise to have both parties carefully review the stated requirements and, if the requirements are acceptable, to sign off on them.

Rule 2: Be realistic; assume that if a requirement can be misinterpreted, it will be misinterpreted. This rule is a variant of Murphy's law, which states that if something can go wrong, it will. In examining the way a requirement is stated, do everything possible to determine how it can be misinterpreted. Ask different staff members to offer their interpretations of the requirement. Ask end-users their interpretation. Determine the views of other people who will be affected by the project; if their opinion of what the requirement should be varies from the end-users' opinion, there may be trouble. If it is a very important project, hire independent experts to review the requirements and see whether their viewpoint corresponds with yours. If these things are done early in the project, you are likely to avoid some nasty surprises midway through the project or at the end.

Rule 3: Be realistic; recognize that there will be changes on your project and that things will not go precisely as anticipated. We have examined this point in detail in this chapter, as well as in the previous chapter, dealing with the definition of needs. The basic lesson to be conveyed here is to avoid excessive rigidity in formulating requirements and to anticipate change.

Rule 4: To as great an extent as possible, include pictures, graphs, physical models, and other nonverbal exhibits in the formulation of requirements. I had my first lesson on the limitations of language some thirty years ago, when I was a sixth-grade student. One day the school principal visited my class, and he set us a challenge: to describe a spiral verbally, without using our hands. I think we did a pretty good job of it, but it was difficult. We would have done a better job if we could have simply drawn a spiral on the blackboard. This lesson was again driven home a couple of years ago, when I carried out a study on how patent examiners determine the technical capabilities of the inventions they review. I interviewed a number of patent examiners, and over and over they told me that the key to doing their job was the drawings that accompany the verbal description of the invention. Several patent examiners stated that a review of the drawings alone gives them almost full knowledge of what an invention can do and what the patent applicant's patent claims are.

The point here is an old one: a picture—or graph, or flow

chart, or mockup model—is worth a thousand words. Engineers and architects have long recognized this in their projects, and the clarification of requirements with blueprints, drawings, and the like, is commonplace in these professions. It is less commonplace—in fact, it is downright rare—in the more mundane, informal, white-collar projects we typically carry out in our organizations. This is a pity, since these nonverbal exhibits can dramatically enhance the clarity of the requirements we are trying to establish.

Rule 5: Establish a system to monitor carefully any changes made to the requirements. Construction companies have long recognized that they would go broke if they did not keep meticulous records of changes made to their projects. Therefore, they have established sytems to keep track of changes. Systems developed for keeping track of changes should address themselves to two basic issues. First, projects are themselves systems—that is, they are made up of interrelated parts. If a change is made to one part, will it have system-wide ripple effects? Remember, the consequences of any given change may be profound and widespread. The second basic issue is that changes have costs associated with them. The costs may be obvious, as when a change requires the disassembly of a piece of hardware and its reassembly in a new way. But the costs may also be more subtle. For example, change always has hidden administrative costs associated with it. There is a strong relationship between these two issues. The greater the system-wide impact of a change, the greater the likelihood that costs associated with the change will be substantial.

The nature of the system developed for tracking changes to project requirements will vary according to the character of the project and the organization in which it is carried out. Large, complex projects require a high degree of formality in tracking changes; otherwise, countless small changes will be lost in the shuffle. With smaller projects, formality can be reduced. In fact, too much paperwork can measurably decrease the productivity of the smaller effort. However, at a minimum—in large projects or small—written change orders should be required. The change order should contain the following information:

- date of the change request
- name of the person requesting the change
- description of the change
- statement of the change's impact on the project
- listing of tasks and staff affected by the change
- estimate of the cost of the change
- signature of the individual making the change request, indicating that this individual is aware of the cost and performance impacts of the requested change

With such a written change order, those desiring changes—whether designers or end-users—are required to take responsibility for their requests. Given this personal assumption of responsibility, they are less likely to make frivolous requests that may have an impact far from frivolous.

Rule 6: Educate project staff and end-users to the problems of specifying requirements. Anyone experienced in working with projects recognizes that one important cause of problems with project requirements is that inexperienced project staff and naive end-users are ignorant of what is involved in generating and meeting requirements. They demonstrate time and again the old maxim that fools rush in where angels fear to tread. End-users may pepper the project team with requests for changes, not realizing the enormous impact these requests may have. Staff may set up requirements in an arbitrary, slipshod way, seeing them more as guidelines for action than as blueprints that need to be followed precisely. The list of mischief that staff and end-users can unwittingly get into is never ending.

To lessen requirements-related problems that are rooted in raw ignorance and naiveté, project staff and end-users should be educated about the needs/requirements life cycle. They should be made aware that requirements serve as the target at which the development of project plans is aimed, so that the quality and viability of the plan are tightly connected to the quality and viability of the requirements. They should be taught that requirements are inherently slippery critters and that changes in them will have an impact on the project budget. Finally, they should be made to view requirements as the provisions of a contract stating what the end-user needs and what the project team has agreed to provide.

Application Prototyping

A project management technique called *application prototyping* is emerging in the software industry. This technique recognizes that with computer software projects—or any other projects that deal largely with intangibles—it is hard to picture concretely what the project should be producing. Consequently, there is a good chance that the final deliverable—based on an amorphous understanding of end-user needs—will not satisfy the end-user. In order to deal with this reality of software projects, application prototyping allows for the dynamic development of requirements rather than demanding that all requirements be cast in iron at the outset of the project. It allows the end-user to play an active role in defining the requirements *as the project is being carried out.*

At the heart of the technique is the concept of iterative prototyping of an intangible deliverable. Let's say that a software development team is contracted to produce a computerized inventory control system for an end-user. Working closely with the end-user, the team identifies end-user needs and from these generates requirements. Then the team begins work on the project, with the objective of quickly putting together a simple prototype of the final deliverable. The first prototype may be nothing more than a set of CRT screen images of a data entry form. When the prototype is completed, it is brought before the end-user, who has an opportunity to see what is being developed early in the project life cycle. After examining the prototype, the end-user may, for example, express general satisfaction with the product but note that it appears as if the emerging system will not process and track incoming inventory items well. The software team then takes account of the end-user input, refines the software, and quickly develops a new, more detailed prototype. Once again the end-user examines the prototype and offers comments and suggestions. The project proceeds in this itera-tive fashion until a final product is developed and handed over to the end-user.

For application prototyping to work effectively, rules for prototyping and requesting improvements to the evolving system must be carefully spelled out; otherwise, the project may never be brought to a conclusion, and costs may get out of hand. For example, how detailed should a given prototype be? How many prototypes should be developed during the course of the proj-ect? What are the limitations on end-user requests for improve-ments to the deliverable? How will the cost impacts of changes to the prototype be calculated?

The advantage of the prototyping approach is obvious. The final deliverable should make the end-user happy, since he or she played a major role in defining what it looks like. This is not a trivial point, since costly rework efforts will have to be undertaken if the deliverable is unsatisfactory, and the project may even have to be redone completely. Another advantage is that application prototyping provides project managers with a methodology for making the intangible a bit more tangible—for dealing proactively with some of the significant problems that arise on amorphous, white-collar, information-age projects.

The disadvantages of application prototyping are also ob-vious. For one thing, there is a risk that heavy involvement of the end-user in defining the product as it evolves will be taken as an invitation for the end-user to change things according to whim. There is also a danger that unless there is a strong com-mitment on the part of both the end-user and project staff to bring the project to a conclusion, the project may drift from prototype to prototype without ever coming to closure.

The application prototyping methodology is very recent; it has not been around long enough to be fully tested across a broad array of projects. In theory, it appears to be a clever step forward in the direction of getting better control over some of the significant problems that arise in relation to the specification of needs. It remains to be seen whether the actual practice of appli-cation prototyping will live up to its theoretical potential. A good book dealing with this methodology is *Application Prototyping: A Requirements Definition Strategy for the 80s* (Boar, 1984).

Conclusion

The writing of good requirements is a formidable task. The pitfalls are bountiful: The requirements may be ambiguous or unrealistic, or they may have no bearing on the user's true needs. They may be too detailed or not detailed enough. They may be too rigid or overly flexible. If the pitfalls are not avoided, problems will arise.

This chapter has shown that there are many things project staff can do to develop good requirements. The single most important step, however, is the simplest: be aware of the role that requirements play in the evolution of a project. Staff should recognize that requirements form the basis of project plans, since the purpose of the plans is to describe how the requirements can be met. If the requirements are deficient, then the project plan is flawed; and if the plan is flawed, then its implementation is defective. An understanding of the connection between requirements and the plan also leads to an appreciation of how modifications to the requirements can yield cost and schedule overruns, since changes in the requirements necessitate changes in the plan.

With a thorough understanding of the importance of requirements, staff will be better able to identify and deal with the many big and little requirements-related problems that *will* arise on their project.

7

Keeping the Project
on Course:
Tools and Techniques
for Planning and Control

Thus far we have focused on two major categories of pitfalls commonly encountered in project management. First, in Chapters Two through Four, we examined organizationally induced problems—problems arising from the very structure of projects and the organizations in which they are carried out. In Chapters Five and Six, we turned our attention toward problems associated with the identification of needs and the specification of requirements. In this and the following chapter, we investigate a third important source of project difficulties: poor planning and control. Project managers, staff, and end-users can be sure that problems in each of these three areas *will* arise; with this knowledge and an understanding of the specific nature of many of these problems, they can avoid stumbling into avoidable pitfalls and can better manage the difficulties they will inevitably encounter.

In the project management literature, probably more attention is directed toward planning and control than any other topic. I suspect this is largely a consequence of the fact that project managers and their staff can exercise a high degree of discretion over how they carry out planning and control activities. It also reflects a philosophy that we should devote most of our study time to learning about things over which we have some influence. On a given project, many things will happen that are out of our hands and beyond our control. An important subcontractor may go bankrupt, our department budget may be slashed in half, the people assigned to us may not have the skills necessary to do a good job. Project managers facing a steady flow of problems arising from outside their realm of control assume a *reactive* posture, *responding* to difficulties as best they can with a limited toolkit of project management techniques and skills. However, with planning and control, wise project managers can turn things to their advantage. They can assume a *proactive* posture, *initiating* actions that will (1) enable them to anticipate what needs to be done in order to carry out a project effectively and (2) help them to make sure things are being undertaken as planned once the project is under way.

Good planning and control are necessary conditions for project success. It is hard to imagine how an unplanned project with no controls could possibly succeed—except, perhaps, through blind luck. Sadly, good planning and control are not sufficient conditions for success. If we want to succeed, we need to be diligent in our planning and control efforts; however, this diligence will not assure success, since, despite our best efforts, surprises may arise that have a devastating impact on our project.

In this chapter, I focus on commonly accepted planning and control practices employed on projects. These practices have evolved over the years, arising chiefly from construction and engineering projects. The techniques described here are relevant to most information-age projects. Their systematic application on projects will help project managers and staff avoid creating problems that should never arise.

The Project Plan

A project plan is basically a road map that tells us how to get from A to B. Typically, we see the plan as the launching point of a project—a beginning, a guide to future developments. However, it is important to recognize that a plan is the consequence of a good deal of effort. As we saw in previous chapters, the plan emerges gradually as needs are defined, requirements are specified, predictions are made about the future, and a tally is undertaken of the resources available to us. Only after these and other matters are mulled over, pieced together, refined, scrapped, reworked, and refined again do we finally encounter a plan that can serve as our road map.

Plans are generally three-dimensional. They focus on time, money, and human and material resources. Planning tools have been developed for each of the three dimensions. The time dimension is handled through schedules. A broad array of scheduling tools—some sophisticated, some simple—are available for use on projects. These tools enable us to determine when different tasks should begin, when milestones will be achieved, and so on. In this chapter, we examine two of the most commonly employed scheduling tools: Gantt charts and scheduling networks.

The money dimension is handled by means of budgets, which lay out for us how our project funds are to be allocated. The need for budgeting is a universal reality in organizations, and we find that most organizations—be they in the private, public, academic, or nonprofit sectors—spend a substantial amount of effort putting together budgets. Although there are universal principles underlying sound budgeting practice, the specific way in which budgets are formulated varies considerably from organization to organization. Budgeting is a very personal thing, reflecting organizational philosophies, attitudes, and structures. In this chapter, we only briefly consider basic budgeting principles; we then devote most of our attention to examining how budget variances can be examined to strengthen project control. In the next chapter, we look at the budgeting issue again when we examine the earned value technique, a cost-accounting technique that is gaining great popularity in project management.

The human and material resource dimension is concerned with how best to allocate our limited resources on projects. Many resource allocation tools exist. In this chapter, we examine resource Gantt charts, resource spreadsheets, resource matrices, and resource loading charts.

Planning and Uncertainty

Mastery of planning tools is extremely helpful in managing projects, but even an expert with good tools cannot create the perfect plan. Planning entails the future, and in dealing with the future we are dealing with uncertainty. A fundamental reality of planning, then, is that it involves uncertainty. This means that our very best plans are estimates, mere approximations of what the future may hold. Sometimes these estimates can be very accurate, as when, after completing work on 999 identical houses, we estimate how long it will take to build the last house in a thousand-unit housing subdivision. Uncertainty here is reduced because we have ample historical experience on which we can base our guesses about the future. More often, though, our estimates are quite rough, because what we want to do has never before been done in precisely the way we need. This is especially true on information-age projects. In carrying out these novel projects, we are to a large extent trailblazers, and the maps we devise (our plans) are much like the maps of the fifteenth-century Portuguese explorers, filled with broad, vague spaces labeled *terra incognita*.

It is important that project managers, staff, and end-users recognize how uncertainty bears on the planning effort. The character of the plan is largely determined by the level of uncertainty of the proposed project. With projects involving low levels of uncertainty, we can create highly detailed plans, because we have a good idea of precisely how the project will proceed. When we are building the thousandth identical unit in a housing development, for example, our plans can specify precisely how the foundation should be poured, where studs should be placed, where nails should be driven, and so on. Because we have built this particular type of house so frequently, few surprises remain in store for us. In fact, in such a situation we would be remiss *not* to plan in great detail, since these details will help us avoid leaving things to chance.

Projects with high levels of uncertainty, in contrast, cannot support this degree of detailed planning, because there is insufficient information on how things will proceed. Consider a project aimed at finding a cure for cancer. The researchers undertaking this project have very little idea of what they will find. How they carry out their work depends, to a large extent, on their step-by-step discoveries, so their project plan must be rather vague and imprecise. Good planning here may mean *phased* planning. For example, a high-risk two-year project may be broken into six planning phases, with detailed planning first undertaken only for phase 1 (months one through four). Then, toward the end of phase 1, detailed planning commences for phase 2, and so on. To force project staff on a highly uncertain project to develop sophisticated, detailed plans for the whole project is an exercise in futility.

We should bear in mind an important distinction between complexity and uncertainty. I have had participants in my project management seminars ask me, "How can you say that there are low levels of uncertainty in building houses and bridges? Even a routine bridge is highly complex and filled with uncertainty."

That is true. Even a routine bridge *is* highly complex. However, if the bridge is truly routine—that is, if bridges of this sort have been built so many times that we have all the steps for constructing them clearly laid out—we will have a precise idea of what we will encounter in our efforts to build it. By definition, then, we are involved in a situation where uncertainty is low.

The difference between uncertainty and complexity is illustrated in Figure 7.1. In both parts of this figure, we are concerned with getting from A to B. In Figure 7.1a, the path from A to B is long, twisting, and *complex*. (This pattern is common on construction projects.) Nonetheless, the path is precisely known, and if we carefully follow our map we will ultimately arrive at B. In Figure 7.1b, we no longer encounter the complexity of Figure 7.1a. It appears as though the route from A to B is rather straightforward. However, we have a problem when we reach the fork in the road. We are not sure which path will get us to B. In fact, in projects where there are truly high levels of uncertainty (for example, in our cancer project), we are not even certain that B exists! This high level of uncertainty is common on information-age projects.

Figure 7.1. Getting from A to B.

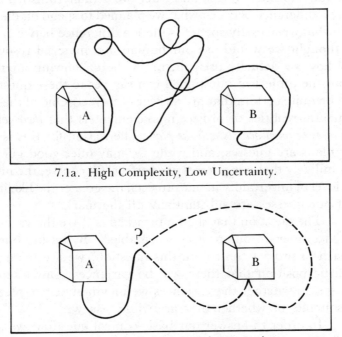

7.1a. High Complexity, Low Uncertainty.

7.1b.   Low Complexity, High Uncertainty.

Project Controls

Project control entails looking at the plan, looking at what is actually happening on the project, and comparing the two. As in project planning, our attention focuses on the three dimensions of time, money, and human and material resources.

The purpose of control is to keep the project on track by keeping track of the project. Control serves a feedback function. For example, a driver is in control of her car when, as it veers slightly to the left, she compensates for this leftward drift by steering slightly to the right. Analogously, a project manager is in control of her project when, say, after learning from her schedule data that a task is falling behind, she directs more resources to the task to put it back on track.

Too often project personnel approach the control function by asking, "Are there variances between the plan and the actuals?" That is, is there a difference between the time we were scheduled to finish a task and when we actually finished it? Is there a difference between what we planned to spend on the task and what we actually spent? Is there a difference between how we thought we would use our human and material resources and how we actually used them? Without knowing anything about the project in question, I can say yes to these questions and be quite certain that my answer is correct. One of the fundamental realities of project management is that *there will be variances between actuals and the plan*. The reason for this is that our plans are guesses, and while we may offer good guesses, it is unlikely that our guesses are perfect. Of course, the higher the level of uncertainty in our projects, the greater the likelihood that our guesses are substantially off the mark.

The question that should be asked is "Are the variances we encounter on our project acceptable?" By basing our approach to project control on this question, we are taking the realistic position that there will be variances. Our attention focuses on whether the variances we inevitably encounter are reasonable, or whether they are wildly askew.

In order to answer our basic control question, we must establish criteria of acceptability for variances. On high-risk projects, with high levels of uncertainty, we typically are willing to accept large variances. For example, on our cancer project, we may be willing to live with variances of 20 percent. That is, although our plan stipulates that a given task will cost $1,000, we may be willing to accept a cost overrun or underrun of up to $200. We accept such large variances because we recognize that our plan entails some rather heroic guesswork on how much it will cost to carry out specific tasks. With low-risk projects— such as routine construction efforts—our criteria of acceptability are much more restrictive, because our knowledge of how things should work out on the project is precise. For example, deviations of more than 2 percent from the plan may be viewed as unacceptable on a routine project.

Given that we have established criteria that define acceptable variances, we do not spend much time fretting over tasks that fall within the acceptable range. Instead, our management efforts are directed at reviewing tasks with variances outside this range. If we spend 8 percent more than planned in March, and our criterion of acceptability is a variance of plus or minus 5 percent, we ask, "What is happening with this task that is resulting in unacceptable overruns?" In using this approach, we are practitioners of *management by exception*, which was discussed briefly in Chapter Three. With this approach, we funnel our energy toward special problems; we do not dissipate it on routine matters.

During the course of the project, then, some variance from the plan is acceptable; as the project comes to termination, however, variance for the entire project should approach zero if we are going to conclude the project close to planned schedule and budget. By the end of the project, the acceptable positive and negative variances that occurred throughout the project should more or less cancel each other out, leaving us with a near zero overall variance if we have done a good planning and control job. Note the distinction here between *acceptable variances* and *unacceptable project overruns*. Practicality and realism suggest that we must be willing to accept some variance from the plan in the day-to-day operation of our project simply because we lack the perfect knowledge that would enable us to predict exactly what will happen. However, although we may accept 5 percent variances from the plan as the project is being carried out, we may not have the luxury of accepting a 5 percent cost or schedule overrun for the project overall. If we are willing to accept such overall overruns, we should build something called *management reserve* into our budget and schedule. This management reserve covers what we view to be an acceptable overrun for the project as a whole.

How Much Planning and Control Is Enough?

Anyone undertaking a planning effort or designing a project control methodology ultimately faces the question "How much planning and control should we engage in?" There is no obvious "best" answer to this question. On the surface, it might seem that we should always implement a major planning and control effort in order to minimize project uncertainty and to be in full control of the project. Our philosophy on this matter might be reflected in statements such as "You can't plan too much" and "A project with weak controls is a project out of control." Unfortunately, planning and control have costs associated with them. The relationship between project costs and the costs of planning and control is illustrated in the following simple formula:

Project Costs = Production Costs + Administrative Costs

What this formula shows is that increases in the costs of planning and control (that is, administrative costs) drive up total project costs. It also illustrates the fact that increases in planning and control costs mean that we are spending smaller and smaller proportions of our project budget on directly productive activities.

What proportion of the project budget should be dedicated to planning and control costs? Ten percent? Twenty percent? Fifty percent? More than fifty percent? How we answer this question is related to a number of important factors.

Project Complexity. How complex is our project? The greater the level of complexity, the greater the need to specify precisely what steps should be taken to carry out the project. In general, highly complex projects need greater planning and control efforts than simple projects.

Project Size. Very large projects require enormous amounts of coordination. On such projects, it is easy for details to get lost in the shuffle, easy for us to lose track of what has been done and what should be done. Consequently, planning and control must be highly formal on large projects, with detailed rules developed that describe how the project should be undertaken. On very large projects—say, in the over $200 million range—administrative costs associated with planning, coordinating, and controlling may constitute from one-half to two-thirds of the total cost of the project. Such a high administrative overhead on a small $10,000 project would be ridiculous, since the small size of the project makes it possible to keep track of things in a more relaxed, less formal way. On small projects, we should start worrying about overplanning and too elaborate controls when the administrative costs associated with planning and control begin edging over the 15 to 25 percent range.

Level of Uncertainty. It is often futile to develop elaborate plans and employ sophisticated control techniques on projects with high levels of uncertainty. As was mentioned earlier, the problem with such projects is that we have very little information about what the future holds. Given great uncertainty, it is guaranteed that the plan—however elaborate it is—will undergo continual modification, so that detailed planning and stringent controls may not work. In fact, they may actually hurt a project if they enforce rigidity on a project that needs flexibility. Projects with low levels of uncertainty can support detailed planning and tight control, because with them we have substantial knowledge of what is necessary to bring them to fruition.

Organizational Requirements. Organizations vary widely in their approach to planning and control. The business press is filled with stories of companies that make it a habit to rush into projects without planning adequately for them, as well as tales of companies that go through an elaborate planning exercise before they make any important decisions. We often read of companies tottering on the brink of bankruptcy because of loose corporate control over operations, as well as companies with such tight control systems that management knows precisely how every penny is spent. In general, organizations with a corporate culture that places emphasis on good corporate-wide planning and control employ good planning and control practices on their projects. The danger here is that management may require you to go through the same planning and control procedures with a $3,000 project as with a $10 million project. Organizations in which corporate culture tolerates sloppy planning and control procedures are likely to foster projects that are poorly planned and controlled.

User-Friendliness of the Planning and Control Tools. If planning and control tools are difficult to learn or cumbersome to use, their employment on projects is likely to reduce project efficiency and drive up administrative costs. With the advent of microcomputers in the workplace, the user-friendliness of many planning and control tools has increased. For example, scores of inexpensive microcomputer-based project scheduling packages have been created that allow individual project managers to develop schedules that a few years ago could only have been developed on mainframes, employing very expensive software and large data processing staffs.

Planning and Control Tools: The Schedule

A major portion of the planning effort entails determining the relationship of different tasks to each other and then scheduling these tasks in such a way that the project is carried out efficiently and logically. A number of tools have been developed over the years that make this undertaking rather routine. Three tools in particular are all that is really necessary to schedule any project, from the simplest to the most complex. They are the work-breakdown structure, the Gantt chart, and the schedule network.

Work-Breakdown Structure

When people begin scheduling a project, the first thing they often do is to generate a list of all the tasks that will be included in the project. First they take a big-picture view of the project and list the major phases that must be addressed. Then they begin adding detail to each phase; they later add detail to the detail. Typically, then, the project schedule takes form in a top-down fashion, starting with the big picture and working down to the minutiae. Most project workers I encounter have been organizing project tasks in this way for years without knowing that the approach they are taking has a fancy name, work-breakdown structure (WBS).

The WBS is nothing more than a top-down formulation of how project tasks fit into the overall project structure. It is an important planning tool because it serves as the basis of the project schedule. The WBS usually takes one of two possible forms. Table 7.1 shows a tablular WBS created for a project to write a spy novel. The hierarchy of tasks is plainly evident in this four-tier WBS. At the highest level is the overall project: to write a spy novel. At the next level down, there are four basic phases (for example, research background material, outline story). Each phase is broken down into tasks (for example, go to library), and each task is further broken down into subtasks (for example, read up on U.S.-Soviet relations). The number of levels needed for a WBS varies according to personal preference and project size. Clearly, very large projects demand more levels than small projects.

Table 7.1. Tabular Work-Breakdown Structure.

Write a Spy Novel

10.0.0 Research background material
    10.1.0 Go to library
        10.1.1 Read up on U.S.-Soviet relations
        10.1.2 Read other spy novels
        10.1.3 Read current periodicals to identify hot topics of interest today
        10.1.4 Locate maps of relevant cities (e.g., Moscow, Washington)
    10.2.0 Interview relevant government officials
        10.2.1 Visit intelligence agencies
        10.2.2 Visit military agencies
        10.2.3 Visit civilian agencies, including FBI and State Department
        10.2.4 Interview local police

11.0.0 Outline story
    11.1.0 Rough out plot
        11.1.1 Establish story theme
        11.1.2 Identify principal characters
        11.1.3 Link story events chronologically
    11.2.0 Refine plot
        11.2.1 Create detailed chart linking characters and events
        11.2.2 Identify chapters to be used in novel

Table 7.1. Tabular Work-Breakdown Structure, Cont'd.

12.0.0 Write story
    12.1.0 Chapter 1
        12.1.1 Kids discover body in the Potomac River
        12.1.2 Body identified as KGB agent
        12.1.3 Frank Masters, FBI agent, put on case
        12.1.4 The Masters family
    12.2.0 Chapter 2
        12.2.1 [And so on, through all the chapters]

13.0.0 Contact publishers
    13.1.0 Identify likely publishers
        13.1.1 Examine *Writer's Guide* to learn of publisher requirements
        13.1.2 Talk to published authors experienced in dealing with publishers
        13.1.3 Contact four likely publishers and have preliminary discussion with editors
    13.2.0 Send three sample chapters to prospective publishers
        13.2.1 Select appropriate chapters
        13.2.2 Send chapters to target publishers
        13.2.3 Follow up with publishers

Figure 7.2 shows a pictorial version of the WBS for the same project to write a spy novel. The WBS in this form looks something like an organization chart. With this format, we can see at a glance the hierarchical relationships of the different pieces of the project to each other.

Sometimes it is useful to include cost estimates for each of the subtasks. When we do this, we have something called a *costed* work-breakdown structure. To find out what the cost of a given level of the work-breakdown structure is, one need merely add together the individual costs of the related items in the next level down. We can estimate the cost for the total project by summing the costs of all the items at the lowest level of the WBS.

Gantt Chart

The Gantt chart allows us to see easily when tasks should begin and when they should end. There are two basic approaches to creating a Gantt chart, and these are pictured in Figure 7.3. In both approaches, tasks (taken from the WBS) are listed on the vertical axis, while time is measured along the horizontal axis.

Figure 7.2. Work-Breakdown Structure in Chart Form.

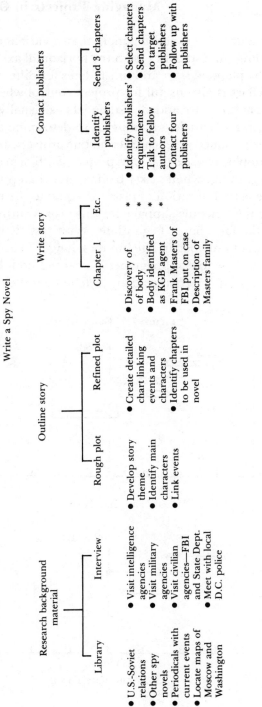

Write a Spy Novel

Research background material

Library
- U.S.-Soviet relations
- Other spy novels
- Periodicals with current events
- Locate maps of Moscow and Washington

Interview
- Visit intelligence agencies
- Visit military agencies
- Visit civilian agencies—FBI and State Dept.
- Meet with local D.C. police

Outline story

Rough plot
- Develop story theme
- Identify main characters
- Link events

Refined plot
- Create detailed chart linking events and characters
- Identify chapters to be used in novel

Write story

Chapter 1
- Discovery of of body
- Body identified as KGB agent
- Frank Masters of FBI put on case
- Description of Masters family

Etc.
- *
- *
- *

Contact publishers

Identify publishers
- Identify publishers' requirements
- Talk to fellow authors
- Contact four publishers

Send 3 chapters
- Select chapters
- Send chapters to target publishers
- Follow up with publishers

Figure 7.3a is nothing more than a variant of a bar chart. By reading time statistics from the horizontal axis, project staff know the planned start and finish dates for different tasks. The Gantt chart is also useful for project control when actual start and finish times are added. It then lets us visually compare our plan with the actuals, enabling us to determine the amount of schedule variance we encounter on our projects. In Figure 7.3a, for example, we see that our project is off schedule from the very beginning, when task 1 begins later than planned. Notice that the actual duration of task 1 is equal to the planned duration, so the schedule slippage for this task is entirely accounted for by the fact that it began late. With task 2, it is clear that the task not only began late but took longer to accomplish than planned. Schedule slippage here is caused both by a late start and sluggish performance that stretched out the task's planned duration.

Figure 7.3. Gantt Chart.

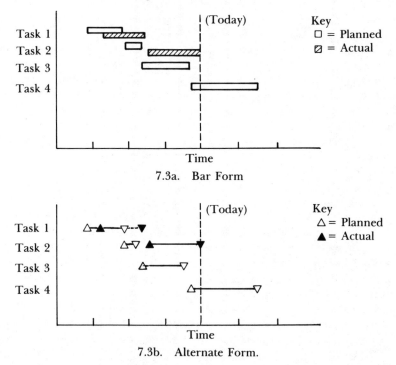

7.3a.   Bar Form

7.3b.   Alternate Form.

Figure 7.3b presents a different approach to the Gantt chart. The basic facts given here are identical to those offered in Figure 7.3a; however, they are presented in a different way. With this approach, planned start dates are pictured as hollow upright triangles and planned finish dates as hollow downward-pointing triangles. Actual start dates are solid upright triangles, and actual finish dates are solid downward-pointing triangles. A comparison of the charts in Figure 7.3 shows that they both tell us the same thing. Once again, in Figure 7.3b, we see that task 1 begins and ends late but that the duration of the task is as planned. Task 2 begins late, stretches out longer than planned, and ends very late.

Gantt charts are widely used for the planning and control of schedules on projects. Many project workers employ them without even knowing that they have a special name. Their popularity lies in their simplicity. No special training is needed to learn how to use them; they do not demand any equipment to make them other than a sheet of graph paper, a pencil, and a ruler. They are easy to understand and are especially useful for examining schedule variance, since they convey project slippage dramatically.

PERT/CPM Schedule Network

The fundamental weakness of Gantt charts is that, while they portray the start and finish dates for tasks, they do not show how schedule changes on a task can have project-wide consequences. That is, Gantt charts look at tasks as if they were independent activities and do not take into account their interconnected nature. In the late 1950s, two techniques were simultaneously developed that allowed project staff to examine the consequences of changes of task start and finish dates on the overall project schedule. One technique, developed for the Navy's Polaris missile program, was called the Program Evaluation and Review Technique (PERT). Another, developed by DuPont, was called the critical path method (CPM). Both approaches are based on flow charts that look similar, but each has a different way of approaching schedule computations. Over the years, countless hours have been spent debating the merits of one approach over the other. Today less and less distinction is being made between the two approaches; in fact, in the microcomputer-based scheduling software that has become popular, a generally accepted PERT/CPM hybrid has emerged that capitalizes on the best features of each approach. I will make no distinction between the two approaches in this chapter.

Building a PERT/CPM Network. The first step in building a PERT/CPM network is to create a WBS for the project. Table 7.2 portrays a very simple WBS for a project to prepare for a picnic.

Table 7.2. Work-Breakdown Structure for Picnic Project.

	Task	*Duration (mins.)*	*Worker*
1.	Start	0	
2.	Make iced tea	15	George
3.	Prepare sandwiches	10	Martha
4.	Prepare fruit	2	Martha
5.	Prepare basket	2	Martha
6.	Gather blankets	2	George
7.	Gather sportsgear	3	Martha
8.	Load car	4	George
9.	Get gas	6	George
10.	Drive to picnic grounds	20	Martha
11.	End	0	

The next step is to create a special kind of flow chart from the information contained in the WBS. What PERT/CPM networks do is incorporate scheduling information into a basic flow chart diagram. This is illustrated in Figure 7.4a. Here the tasks listed in the WBS are placed into boxes, the boxes are laid out according to the sequence in which they should occur, and their relationships with each other are shown with lines. For example, the line connecting ''Prepare sandwiches'' and ''Prepare fruit'' shows that we begin preparing the fruit only after we have completed our sandwiches. The two lines feeding into ''Prepare basket'' show that we cannot begin work on the picnic basket until we have made the iced tea and finished preparing the fruit.

In each box that represents a task, the amount of time it takes to complete the task is given in the upper-right-hand corner. Making iced tea, for example, takes fifteen minutes.

The Critical Path. An important concept necessary for an understanding of PERT/CPM networks is that of the *critical path*. The critical path in a schedule network is the path that takes the longest time to complete. In Figure 7.4a, consider the two paths that take you from "Start" to "Prepare Basket." The upper path, "Make iced tea," takes fifteen minutes to complete, while the lower path, which is composed of two tasks ("Prepare sandwiches" and "Prepare fruit"), can be completed in twelve minutes. Given the way the network is drawn, the longest time that can elapse between "Start" and "Prepare Basket" is fifteen minutes. This means that the lower path has three minutes of slack built into it. Since the critical path is always the one that takes the longest to complete, the critical path has no slack at all. In fact, if there is schedule slippage along the critical path, the slippage will be reflected in the project as a whole. Thus, if a task on the critical path takes three minutes longer to complete than anticipated, the overall project schedule will slip by three minutes. It is this feature of the critical path—its inflexibility with regard to slippage of schedule—that gives it its name. Because activities off the critical path have some slack associated with them, they can tolerate some slippage in schedule.

In Figure 7.4a, the critical path for the project is portrayed by a double line. To find out how long the project takes to complete, one need merely add together the times it takes to accomplish each of the tasks on the critical path. In our example, the time needed to accomplish the whole project is fifty minutes $(15 + 2 + 3 + 4 + 6 + 20$ minutes$)$.

Noncritical Tasks and Slack Time. Because noncritical tasks have slack associated with them, there is some flexibility in scheduling their start times. As we have seen, the lower path—between "Start" and "Prepare basket"—has three minutes of slack. Consequently, we need not begin to prepare the sandwiches until three minutes into the project. If we begin

Figure 7.4. Activity-in-Node PERT/CPM Network.

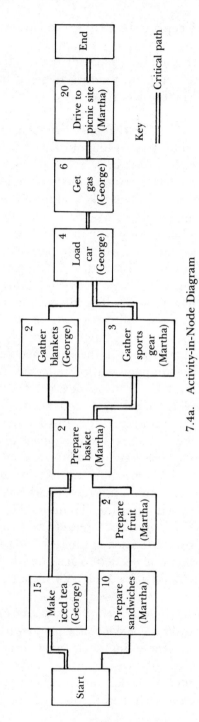

7.4a. Activity-in-Node Diagram

Task	Early Start	Late Start	Slack
Make iced tea	0	0	0
Prepare sandwiches	0	3	3
Prepare fruit	10	13	3
Prepare basket	15	15	0
Gather blankets	17	18	1
Gather sports gear	17	17	0
Load car	20	20	0
Get gas	24	24	0
Drive to picnic site	30	30	0

7.4b.   Calculating Slack.

sandwich preparation at the three-minute mark, we can still complete the project in the allotted time. However, if we begin sandwich preparation at, say, the four-minute mark, we will cause the overall project schedule to slip by one minute.

Earliest and Latest Start Time. Calculating the earliest and latest start times for projects is easy to do. To calculate earliest start times, we begin at the left of the PERT/CPM network and work our way to the right. First we calculate the earliest start times for tasks on the critical path. "Make iced tea" starts at time 0, "Prepare basket" at time 15, "Gather sports gear" at time 17, "Load car" at time 20, "Get gas" at time 24, and "Drive to picnic site" at time 30. After earliest start times for critical tasks have been calculated, we turn to calculating earliest start times for noncritical tasks. Again we move from left to right. "Prepare sandwiches" can begin as early as time 0, "Prepare fruit" at time 10, and "Gather blankets" at time 17.

To calculate latest start times we work from right to left. Once again, we first concentrate on the critical path. Since the project takes 50 minutes to complete, the latest time to start "Drive to picnic site" is at time 30 (that is, $50 - 20$), to start "Get gas" is at time 24 (that is, $30 - 6$), to start "Prepare basket" is at time 15, and to start "Make iced tea" is at time 0. Note that the latest start times are identical to the earliest start times. This is always the case with tasks on the critical path; there is no flexibility in when we start tasks.

To calculate latest start times for noncritical tasks, we also work leftward. Consider the noncritical task "Gather blankets." The activity that occurs after "Gather blankets" is the critical task "Load car," which we have determined should start no later than at time 20. Since "Gather blankets" consumes 2 minutes of time, its latest start time is at time 18 (that is, $20 - 2$). With similar logic, the latest start time for "Prepare fruit" is at time 13; for "Prepare sandwiches," at time 3.

Slack for individual tasks is calculated by subtracting earliest start time from latest start time. For example, the latest start time for "Prepare fruit" is time 13, while its earliest start time is time 10. Slack for this task is $13 - 10$, or 3. This means that we have three minutes of breathing space in carrying out the task. However, as a project is carried out and slack time is consumed on individual tasks, the slack left over for the remaining tasks is reduced. If we do not finish preparing sandwiches until time 12, we have consumed two time units of slack, which means that the earliest time we can start "Prepare fruit" is time 12 and the latest start time is 13, leaving us with only one unit of slack (13 – 12) for "Prepare fruit."

Information on the earliest start time, latest start time, and slack for the picnic project is provided in tabular form in Figure 7.4b.

Resources and Network Configuration. The actual configuration of a PERT/CPM network is heavily dependent upon the amount of resources that can be devoted to the project. For example, the more people we have available, the more parallel activities we are capable of conducting. In our example of preparing for a picnic, we find that five activities could be conducted concurrently if George and Martha had three helpers. One individual could be making the iced tea, another preparing the sandwiches, a third preparing the fruit, a fourth gathering blankets, and a fifth gathering the sports gear. Given these circumstances, we have a different PERT/CPM network than the one portrayed in Figure 7.4.

Activity-in-Node Versus Activity-on-Arrow Networks. The kind of PERT/CPM network we have built in Figure 7.4 is called an *activity-in-node network.* Another popular approach is the *activity-on-arrow network.* This second approach is illustrated in Figure 7.5. Unlike the activity-in-node approach, which puts tasks into boxes, the activity-on-arrow approach places the tasks on the arrows that connect *events* (the circled numbers in Figure 7.5). Events represent either the beginning or the end of a task. Thus, in Figure 7.5, event 3 represents both the end of task $2 \rightarrow 3$ ("Prepare fruit") and task $1 \rightarrow 3$ ("Make iced tea") and the beginning of task $3 \rightarrow 4$ ("Prepare basket").

With the activity-on-arrow approach, we sometimes have occasion to create dummy tasks, tasks that consume no resources.

Figure 7.5. Activity-on-Arrow PERT/CPM Network.

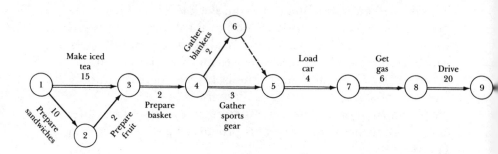

Task 6→5 in Figure 7.5 is such a dummy task, created because to get from event 4 to event 5 we wish to undertake two tasks: "Gather blankets" and "Gather sports gear." Both of these tasks cannot be described as 4→5, since this would lead to confusion as to whether 4→5 represents "Gather blankets" or "Gather sports gear." Consequently, one of the tasks ("Gather blankets") is arbitrarily given the assignation 4→6, to distinguish it from 4→5. To do so, however, requires the creation of dummy task 6→5.

Which approach is superior, the activity-in-node or activity-on-arrow PERT/CPM chart? Whichever approach you feel more comfortable with. Although the project management literature is filled with discussions of the relative merits of one approach over the other, the advantages of one over the other are marginal. Old-timers are apt to have learned the activity-on-arrow approach when they studied PERT/CPM networking twenty years ago, and they are usually more comfortable with this approach. With the recent burst of scheduling software produced for microcomputers, the current trend is clearly toward the activity-in-node approach, simply because this approach is far easier to portray on a computer screen than the arrow approach.

Usefulness of the PERT/CPM Network for Planning and Control. PERT/CPM networks are clearly useful for project planning, because they force project staff to identify carefully the tasks that need to be undertaken and to determine precisely the relationships of the tasks to each other. Given the tendency of project staff to rush into a project without giving much thought to what needs to be done to carry out the project effectively, this is no mean accomplishment. PERT/CPM networks are also useful in planning because they allow planners to develop what-if scenarios, by which planners can determine the impact on the overall project schedule of slippages and speed-ups of individual tasks.

Schedule networks are less useful as control tools. For one thing, continual updating of the network can be quite burdensome. For another, the networks do not graphically show schedule variances, as do Gantt charts; to see variances, you cannot simply superimpose an updated PERT/CPM chart over the original.

Planning and Control Tools: The Budget

One major responsibility of many project managers is developing and adhering to a budget for the project. Often they will be rated a success or failure as project managers according to whether the project comes in under budget, on budget, or over budget. Overshooting the budget can have serious consequences for project managers and the organizations in which they work. Consider a project that is funded through a contract: a cost overrun may lead to litigation, penalties, and financial losses for the performing organization. If the project is funded internally, an overrun may lead to a serious drain of organizational resources.

In view of the importance of budgeting, it is not surprising to find that most organizations focus much of their management attention on that area. Consequently, most organizations have well-developed budgeting techniques that are custom-made for the organization's particular environment and operating style.

Components of the Budget

Project costs are typically comprised of four components: direct labor costs, overhead, fringe benefits, and auxiliary costs. *Direct labor costs* are determined by multiplying the workers' hourly (or monthly) wages by the amount of time that they are expected to spend on the project. In most service projects, which are not capital-intensive, direct labor costs are the largest single component of project costs.

Overhead costs are the typical expenses incurred in maintaining the environment in which the workers function. Included here are the costs of office supplies, the electric bill, rent, and—frequently—secretarial expenses. It should be noted that what is treated as an overhead expense in one organization may be given different treatment in another. In an organization that does not typically use secretarial service, for example, secretarial expenses might be included as a direct labor expense or even as an auxiliary expense. Overhead costs tend to be relatively fixed in relation to direct labor costs. For example, if over the long run labor costs increase by 50 percent, overhead costs similarly tend to increase by 50 percent.

Fringe benefits are nonsalary benefits derived by the worker from the organization. They include the employer's contribution to the worker's Social Security payments. Depending on the organization, they may also include employer contributions to the worker's health insurance, life insurance, profit-sharing plan, stock options, pension plan, bonuses, and university tuition. Fringe benefit expenses are also directly proportional to direct labor costs.

Auxiliary expenses are project-specific expenses that the organization does not incur with any obvious regularity. Project travel expenses, purchases of special equipment and materials, computer time, consultant fees, and report reproduction costs are typical items in this category.

On many projects, knowledge of labor costs enables us to make good estimates of total project costs. For information-age projects, on which knowledge worker salaries are often the most important component of the budget, estimating the budget is closely tied to estimating the amount of labor needed to carry out project tasks. Overhead costs and fringe benefit expenses are linked to direct labor costs; therefore, if we know what the direct labor costs are, we can readily estimate total project costs, where auxiliary costs have been netted out. If we also know what auxiliary costs will be, we have a good estimate of total project costs.

Table 7.3 illustrates a typical project cost-estimating procedure for a company whose overhead averages 65 percent of direct labor costs and whose fringe benefits average 25 percent of direct labor costs plus overhead expenses. These overhead and fringe benefit figures are determined by accountants and/or auditors, who calculate them from data in the organization's accounting records.

Table 7.3. Estimating Project Expenses.

Project manager (500 hours at $19 per hour)..........	$ 9,500	
Analyst (1,000 hours at $14 per hour)................	14,000	
Technicians (200 hours at $10 per hour).............	2,000	
Total Labor expenses.....................................		$25,500
Overhead (65 percent of labor)......................	16,575	
Total labor plus overhead expenses...........................		42,075
Fringes (25 percent of labor plus overhead)............	10,519	
Subtotal..		52,594
Transportation (4 trips at $600 per trip)..............	2,400	
Microcomputers (2 microcomputers at $3,500).........	7,000	
Printing and reproduction........................	1,000	
Total auxiliary expenses.................................		10,400
Total project expenses.....................................		$62,994

Table 7.3 shows that in the case of our hypothetical company, direct labor, overhead, and fringe benefit expenses are $52,594. This figure turns out to be 2.06 times greater than direct labor costs alone ($25,500). Thus, in estimating project costs, a project manager in this company can reasonably guess that project costs (excluding auxiliary expenses) will be somewhat more than twice as great as direct labor costs. Of course, in making the final estimate of total costs, the project manager must include auxiliary costs, which may or may not be substantial, depending on the specific nature of the project.

Management Reserve

One unfortunate reality of project management is the ever-looming threat that project costs will be exceeded. To cope with this threat, project managers commonly build some "fat" into their cost estimates. One frequently used procedure is to make as realistic an estimate as possible of project costs and then multiply this estimate by some "fudge factor" in order to take into account unanticipated problems. Building a management reserve of 5 or 10 percent is typical on projects with low levels of uncertainty; with high-risk projects, the management reserve percentage may be much greater.

Not everyone espouses the creation of a management reserve. Some project management experts are opposed to this concept, arguing that management reserves encourage cost overruns and undermine the discipline of the tight purse.

Budget Control

As was mentioned earlier in this chapter, project staff can expect to encounter variances on their projects—deviations of actual performance from the plan. The important thing is not whether a variance exists but what its dimensions are. If a deviation lies outside an acceptable range, the variance should be flagged and its causes should be investigated.

Table 7.4 gives an example of how variance analysis can be used in controlling the budget. This table portrays a monthly budget report for a small project. As the report states, we are in the sixteenth month of a twenty-month project. The second column of the report, "Amount Previously Claimed," tells how much was actually spent on the project up to, but not including, the month being reported. The third column, "Amount Budgeted," shows how much was budgeted for the project for the report month. The fourth column, "Amount Claimed This Period," gives information on actual expenditures for the report month. The fifth and sixth columns, "Variance" and "Percent Variance," calculate the difference between budgeted and actual expenditures for the report month. (Values inside parentheses represent negative variances, and those without parentheses indicate positive variances. Asterisks indicate that the variance is greater than 10 percent.)

The seventh and eighth columns provide data on budgeted cumulative expenditures (including the report month) and actual cumulative expenditures (including the report month), respectively. The last columns, "Variance from Total" and "Percent Variance," show the difference between columns seven and eight. They give the cumulative variance for the project to date.

Table 7.4. Tracking the Budget.

Expenditure Category	Amount Previously Claimed	Amount Budgeted	Amount Claimed This Period	Variance	% Variance	Cumulative Total, Budgeted	Cumulative Total, Actual	Variance From Total	% Variance
Salary	28,716	1,500	1,716	(216)[a]	14.4*	30,000	30,432	(432)	1.4
Transportation	536	150	0	150	100.0*	800	536	264	33.0*
Supplies	2,418	300	0	300	100.0*	4,000	2,418	1,582	39.6*
Consultants	99	0	0	0	0.0	500	99	401	80.2*
Overhead	17,804	975	1,115	(140)	14.4*	19,500	18,919	581	3.0
Fee	3,965	248	226	22	8.9	4,950	4,192	758	15.3*
Total	53,538	3,173	3,057	116	3.7	59,750	56,596	3,154	5.3

Date: Month 16 of a 20-Month Project.
[a] Amounts in parentheses are negative variances.
*Variance > 10%.

A quick perusal of Table 7.4 suggests that things are going pretty well for this project. The total variance for the report month is positive ($116, or 3.7 percent), and the total variance for cumulative expenditures to date is also positive ($3,154, or 5.3 percent), indicating that the project is coming in slightly under budget. However, there are a couple of items in the budget report that warrant closer inspection. Note, for example, the following two concerns.

Why is the variance for supplies so large ($1,582, or 39.6 percent)? This positive variance might suggest that project staff have been able to procure supplies at a discount price, leading to cost savings for the project. However, it might also suggest that the project schedule is slipping—that is, supply costs might be low simply because supplies have not yet been purchased.

Why has only $99 been expended for consultants when $500 was budgeted? On the bright side, cost-conscious project staff may have been able to answer project questions through internal resources that otherwise would have required outside expertise. On the negative side, the positive variance for consultant expenditures could be a consequence of schedule slippage: consultants have not been paid because they have not yet been used.

Overall, this budget suggests that the project is reasonably under control from the perspective of costs. In view of the fact that the project is nearing its end (remember, we are in the sixteenth month of a twenty-month project), we might have some concern about the 5.3 percent overall positive variance, because it might suggest that we have not yet accomplished all we planned to accomplish. A quick perusal of the project schedule (in particular, the Gantt chart) should allow us to see whether we have schedule slippage. If no slippage is revealed, we are in good shape and can expect to see some cost savings on the project.

Cumulative Cost Curve

A common practice in project planning and control is to create a chart of cumulative expenditures for the project. Cost curves for planned and actual expenditures are created by adding each month's expenditures to the previous reporting period's expenditures. In this way, smooth, climbing, nondecreasing cost curves are generated, as illustrated in Figure 7.6. The height of a curve represents total costs to date for a given point of time. For example, the height of the curve of planned expenditures at the very end of the project represents total budgeted costs.

Figure 7.6. Cumulative Cost Curve.

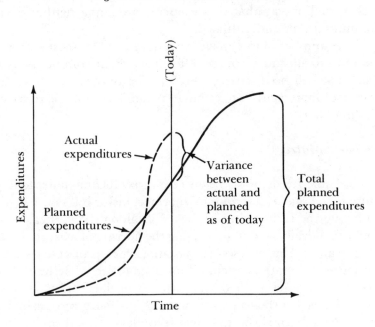

Cumulative cost curves are useful for monitoring cost variances at a glance. The difference in height between the curve for planned expenditures and the curve for actual expenditures represents the monetary value of variance at any given time. Ideally, the curve for actual expenditures looks very much like the curve for planned expenditures.

Planning and Control Tools:
Human and Material Resources

The primary goal of human and material resource planning is the efficient and effective allocation of resources to a project. The fundamental problem that resource planners must deal with is resource scarcity; the need for resources usually outstrips their availability. In view of the reality of resource scarcity, planners must carefully match available resources with project tasks. In matrix organizations, where many projects are carried out concurrently, this effort can become very complex as planners try to assign resources to meet task needs in many different projects in such a way that the resources are being neither over-committed nor underutilized.

A number of tools have been developed to assist resource planners to allocate resources effectively. Four commonly used tools that will be discussed here are the resource matrix, the resource Gantt chart, the resource spreadsheet, and the resource loading chart.

Resource Matrix

Table 7.5 depicts a resource matrix. Its function is to link human and material resources to project tasks. It is constructed by listing the tasks found in the WBS along the vertical axis, and listing available resources along the horizontal axis. In Table 7.5, we are looking at resource allocations for a project to develop a science and math curriculum for a small school system. The WBS has been simplified for purposes of illustration.

Table 7.5 shows us who assumes primary responsibility for a task (P) and who assumes secondary responsibility (S). For example, in the task to design a preliminary curriculum, the chief responsibility for carrying out the task lies with the curriculum specialists, with methodologists, science specialists, and math specialists assuming a supporting role.

Development of a resource matrix is a wise first step in determining how resources should be allocated. The matrix can be put together in a very short period of time and can serve as a guide for developing more sophisticated resource management tools.

Resource Gantt Chart

The resource matrix shows only resource allocations for tasks; it does not show how these resources are allocated over

Table 7.5. Resource Matrix.

Resources

Tasks	Methodologists	Curriculum Specialists	Evaluators	Science Specialists	Math Specialists	Printing Facilities	Mainframe Computer
Identify Needs	S	P					
Establish Requirements		P					
Design Preliminary Curriculum	S	P		S	S		
Evaluate Design	S	S	P				
Develop Science Curriculum		S		P			
Develop Math Curriculum		S			P		
Test Integrated Curriculum	S	S	P				S
Print and Distribute Findings		S				P	

P = Primary responsibility
S = Secondary responsibility

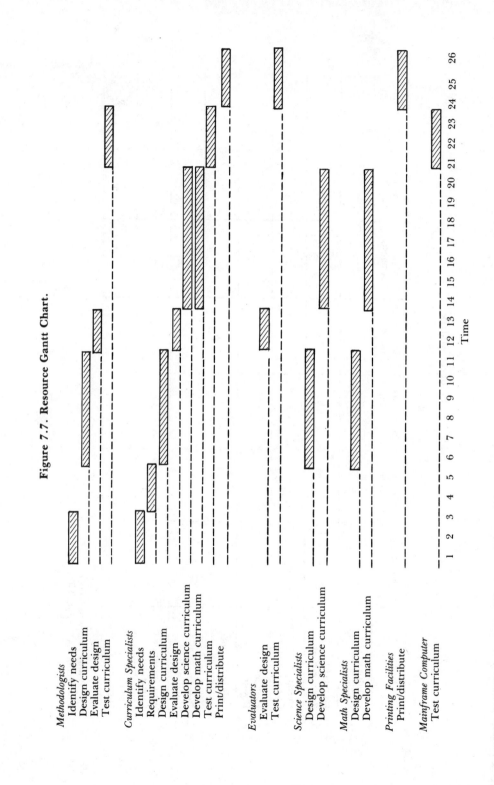

Figure 7.7. Resource Gantt Chart.

time. This is achieved by means of a resource Gantt chart, as pictured for our curriculum development project in Figure 7.7. As can be seen from this figure, the resource Gantt chart shows us how each of our resources should be allocated, task by task, over time. The chart allows us to see at a glance how the resources will be distributed throughout the life of the project. Like the conventional Gantt chart discussed earlier, the resource Gantt enables us to *track* resource allocations as well as plan them. Although I have not done so here, variances can be pictured by juxtaposing actual allocations alongside planned allocations.

Resource Spreadsheet

The resource spreadsheet shows in tabular form the information contained in the graphical resource Gantt chart. Table 7.6 illustrates an aggregated resource spreadsheet for the curriculum development project. It shows how many units of a resource are needed on the project for different periods of time. By summing up the resource requirements across all resources for each time unit, we can calculate total resource requirements for the project over time (see the "Total" row).

Given the widespread proliferation of microcomputer-based electronic spreadsheets, resource spreadsheets are very popular among project managers, since they are easy to develop and maintain. By computerizing a resource spreadsheet, project staff can easily create many different what-if scenarios, allowing them to determine the impact of different configurations of resource allocations and select the best configuration.

Resource Loading Chart

The resource loading chart pictures the project life cycle from a resource consumption perspective. It shows how at the early stages of a project, when we are gearing up to get under way, relatively few resources are employed; at the middle stage, we are moving full steam ahead in using resources; and at the end of the life cycle, our resource consumption winds down.

A resource loading chart for the curriculum development project is shown in Figure 7.8. The chart is easily constructed

Table 7.6. Resource Spreadsheet.

																Time											
	1	**2**	**3**	**4**	**5**	**6**	**7**	**8**	**9**	**10**	**11**	**12**	**13**	**14**	**15**	**16**	**17**	**18**	**19**	**20**	**21**	**22**	**23**	**24**	**25**	**26**
Methodologist	1.5	1.5	1.5																							
Curriculum Specialists	1	1	1	1	1	1	1	1	1	1	1	1	1	1	1	1	1	1	1	1	1	1	1	1	1	1
Evaluators												2	2								2	2	2			
Science Specialists						.75	.75	.75	.75	.75	.75	2	2	2	2	2	2	2	2	2						
Math Specialists						.75	.75	.75	.75	.75	.75			2	2	2	2	2	2	2						
Printing Facilities																								.3	.3	.3
Mainframe Computer																					.1	.1	.1			
Total	2.5	2.5	2.5	1	1	3.5	3.5	3.5	3.5	3.5	3.5	5	5	5	5	5	5	5	5	5	3.1	3.1	3.1	1.3	1.3	1.3

from the "Total" data garnered from the resource spreadsheet. The area under the curve has a physical interpretation. It represents total person-days (or person-weeks, or person-hours, or computer-days, or CAT scan–hours) of effort consumed by the project. Note that our resource loading chart in Figure 7.8 profiles *actual* resource allocations, as well as planned, so that we can monitor variances. In general, if the area under the "actual" curve is much larger than the area under the "planned" curve, we have obviously dedicated more person-days to the project than planned. If the area under the "actual" curve is smaller than the area under the "planned" curve, we have consumed fewer person-days of resources than planned. Resource variance is at a minimum when the area under the two curves is equal or nearly equal.

Figure 7.8. Resource Loading Chart.

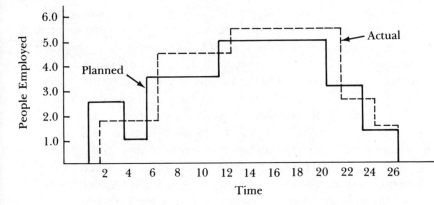

Resource loading charts are popular in managing projects because they simplify the resource control effort. To illustrate this, consider the "actual" versus "planned" curves in Figure 7.8. A comparison of the two curves shows that we were somewhat delayed in beginning to use needed resources on our project. However, by using more resources than planned later on in the project, we are able to make up for some of our earlier deficiencies. Note that the total number of person-days expended in carrying out the project is slightly more than originally planned. Does this mean that we have a cost overrun on the project? Not necessarily. The principal deficiency of the resource loading chart is that it provides us with only highly aggregated information on resource consumption. It tells us nothing about the quality or price of the individual resources. So, although the actuals in Figure 7.8 suggest that more person-days were dedicated to the project than planned, this may not translate into higher project costs *if the resources used to undertake the project had a lower unit cost than originally planned.* In order to find out the impact of increases of person-days on the project budget, one would have to look directly at budget figures.

Resource Leveling

As was stated earlier, the chief concern of resource planners is to allocate human and material resources efficiently and effectively; that is, to assign the right resources to the appropriate tasks in such a way that they are neither overcommitted nor underutilized. This is no easy accomplishment, particularly when a number of projects are being undertaken concurrently, each with its own resource requirements that have been developed independently of the resource requirements of sister projects. For example, we may find that, by random chance, four projects have scheduled the staff artist to work on their projects on the same day. Unless the artist can be cut into four functioning pieces, he will not be able to meet the scheduled requirements for all the projects. Yet two weeks later, the artist may find no demand for his services. The artist faces a feast-or-famine situation common on projects. Anyone working on a project that requires occasional access to the corporate central computer often faces this kind of problem. It seems that just at the moment you want to use the computer, everyone else in the company has a similar urge, tying it up at a crucial moment in your project; yet when you have no need of the computer, it sits idle.

Resource leveling is a concept that applies to most project situations. With resource leveling, planners recognize that something has to give when there are dramatic ups and downs in the demand for limited resources—and that "something" is the project schedule. Resource leveling requires that task schedules be adjusted to create a smooth, consistent demand for resources. If it looks as though George will be overcommitted to project work in December, perhaps a project manager who wants to use him in December will have to reschedule her project so that she can obtain George in November, when George is available.

Resource leveling brings us face to face with the realization that there are trade-offs between schedules and resource utilization. If project planners plan a project purely on the basis of optimizing the schedule, it is likely that resources will not be employed efficiently. On the other hand, planning a project in order to optimize resource utilization is likely to lead to sub-optimization of the schedule. On some projects—for example, projects to develop military hardware—it is often more important to optimize schedule performance than resource utilization. On most projects, however, resource constraints force us to engage in resource leveling, where task scheduling is carried out to accommodate the availability of our precious human and material resources, not the other way around.

Graphical Control of Projects

I have covered the basic principles of project planning and control in this chapter and have discussed the most commonly used planning and control tools. At this point, I will show how these principles and some of the most crucial tools can be brought together to provide project staff with a very powerful methodology for controlling projects.

It should be obvious that if project managers focus all their attention on the project budget, and ignore scheduling and resource utilization issues, they will have a seriously flawed image of what is happening on the project. They will be like the blind men in the old parable, each of whom had a limited and therefore distorted view of what an elephant looks like. For example, when looking over the monthly budget progress reports, project managers may be delighted to see that budget variances

Figure 7.9. Graphical Control of Projects.

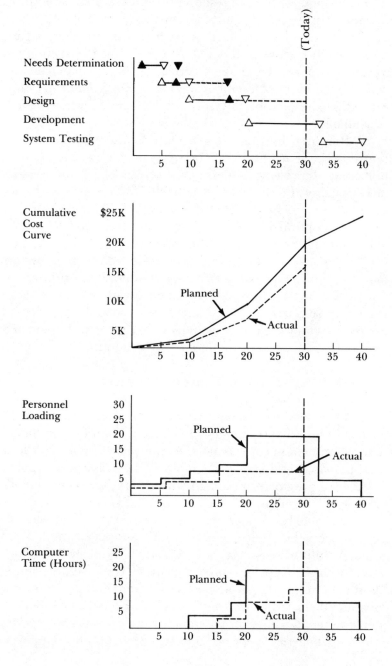

Case A

Figure 7.9. Graphical Control of Projects. Cont'd.

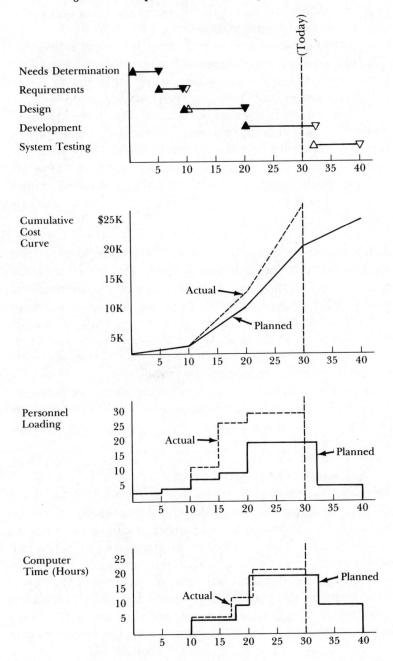

Case B

are nearly zero. Of course, they may be in serious trouble, because budget variance data tell them little or nothing about whether tasks are being completed on time. Similarly, if they look only at the schedule, or only at resource utilization, they will have an incomplete image of project progress. In order to have a complete overview of the project, they must examine schedule, budget, and resource issues simultaneously.

The most effective way of doing this is to place a graphical review of schedule performance (Gantt chart), budget performance (cumulative cost curve), and resource allocations (resource loading chart) on a single sheet of paper, so that project staff can easily compare schedule, budget, and resource information. This has been done in Figure 7.9, which portrays two different project scenarios, case A and case B.

In looking at the Gantt chart for case A, we see immediately that there is serious trouble. The project began according to schedule, but each task is taking longer to accomplish than originally estimated. That schedule delays are occurring because not enough workers are available is reflected in the personnel loading chart, which shows consistent underavailability of project staff. Because staff are not being employed in the numbers originally anticipated, the project is running under budget, a fact that is seen in the cumulative cost curve. The material resource loading chart, showing computer usage, reflects delays in the project: the computer is not being fully utilized because the system development task, which is computer-intensive, has not yet begun.

In case B, we have a dramatically different situation. Here we see from the Gantt chart that the project is on schedule. If the project manager looks no further than the schedule, he will likely think that the project is doing just fine. However, we see from the budget data and the resource loading charts that the project is being kept on schedule at great cost. In fact, a particularly ominous piece of information emerging from the cumulative project budget chart is the knowledge that more has *already* been spent on the project than was budgeted for the project overall! This project is facing a serious cost overrun. The charts in case B illustrate a classic "crashing" scenario; extra resources are thrown into a project to keep it on schedule.

All project managers should use Gantt, cumulative cost, and resource loading charts in the way presented here for project control. When viewed individually, the charts will offer easily understood information on schedule, budget, and resource utilization variances. When viewed collectively, they provide managers with immediate and full insight regarding their project's course. With these valuable, comprehensive insights, project managers can make course correction decisions based on a full view of the project's status rather than on a keyhole glimpse provided by bits and pieces of scattered data. What makes this approach doubly attractive is the fact that these charts are easy to put together. If the required planning and control data have been collected, the charts can be drawn freehand, or by means of a computer, in a matter of minutes.

8

Handling Special Problems and Complex Projects

Chapter Seven covered the basic planning and control material addressed in most courses and texts on project management. The concepts and tools discussed there are now well-accepted standards. In this chapter, I look closely at a number of specialized issues, topics that are crucial to many project managers but are often overlooked in the project management literature or in courses. They are:

- planning and control on large projects
- planning and control of multiple projects
- planning and control for contracted projects
- planning and control with bureaucratic milestones

Planning and Control on Large Projects

Someone with a first-rate track record in managing small projects may be a failure at managing large ones. By the same token, someone who has demonstrated great skill in undertaking large projects may have great difficulty in carrying out small ones. There are some fundamental differences in the requirements of large and small projects that translate into differences in how they should be managed.

Before looking at these differences, we should first investigate what we mean by small and large projects. There are no clear-cut boundaries separating the two, and to a large extent our notion of what is small and what is large is colored by what we are accustomed to. At one of my project management seminars, an Air Force major said to me, "You keep talking about $10 million projects as if they were a big deal. Where I come from, $10 million is pocket money."

One way to get a grasp of the differences between small and large projects is to look at obvious extremes and to determine whether there are features in the two extremes that would distinguish their management requirements. A $5,000 project that occupies two workers for one month is an obvious example of a small project. At the other end of the spectrum, the multibillion-dollar project to put humans on the moon clearly falls into the domain of very large projects.

What are some basic characteristics of the small project? It employs very few human and material resources; it is short-term; and its focus is rather narrow—it deals with a small piece of the whole range of activities an organization carries out. The operational details associated with such a project lie well within the grasp of most project managers, so that the need to spell out these details formally is small. In fact, because of the administrative costs associated with formally spelling out and keeping track of the details, there is a danger that unnecessarily large sums will be spent on planning and tracking.

What are some basic characteristics of the large multibillion-dollar project? It employs huge amounts of human and material resources; it is long-term; and its focus is quite broad—in fact, a discrete organization (called a program office) is often set up to handle the project. With this large project, there is so much to keep track of that a formal, well-specified planning and tracking system must be established to keep on top of planned and unplanned developments. More than half of the project budget may be dedicated to administrative matters associated with formal planning and control.

The Need for Formality in Planning and Controlling Large Projects

While the planning and control techniques discussed in Chapter Seven work well on large projects as well as small ones, the discussion of these techniques assumed that they would be used rather flexibly, which is perfectly appropriate on smaller projects. For example, in answer to the question "How many levels should the work-breakdown structure contain?" a reasonable answer is "Whatever the project manager is comfortable with and whatever seems workable." However, this degree of flexibility in defining the WBS is not viable on a very large project, where there might be 100 task leaders, each creating his or her piece of a super-WBS for the whole project. Each of these task leaders must be given specific, formal instructions on how the WBS should be constructed; otherwise, the results of their efforts will not fit together into a cohesive super-WBS. Let me illustrate this point by describing the requirements for building a WBS on a large government military project. I have, of course, greatly simplified the procedure for purposes of illustration.

On a large military project, the WBS is built from the bottom up. This is illustrated in Table 8.1. At the bottom level of the WBS (called the "level of effort" here), formal instructions may require that each item be constructed in such a way as to represent about 100 person-hours (2.5 person-weeks) of effort. Ten of these items taken together constitute a work package, the next level up in the WBS. Thus, a work package reflects about 1,000 person-hours (.5 person-years) of effort. Ten work packages in turn comprise a subtask, which, as a consequence, represents about 10,000 person-hours (5 person-years) of effort. Extending this logic to higher levels of the WBS, it can be seen that a six-level WBS represents a total of about 10 million person-hours (5,000 person-years) of effort.

Table 8.1. Formal Work-Breakdown Structure.

Level 1	Program				10 million person-hours
Level 2		Project			1 million person-hours
Level 3			Task		100,000 person-hours
Level 4				Subtask	10,000 person-hours
Level 5				Work Package	1,000 person-hours
Level 6				Level of Effort	100 person-hours

Unfortunately, one side effect of the need for increased formality is a proliferation of paper on large projects, in order to maintain communications among project staff. Consider, for example, that even a minor change on a small task may require that notices of the change be sent to fifteen or twenty project workers affected by the change. On a typical very large project, thousands of changes are made each year, necessitating the generation of millions of pieces of paper—which further requires the creation of a mechanism to make sure that the paper arrives at its intended destination, the establishment of additional procedures for storage and retrieval of this information, and so forth. It should come as no surprise, then, that such a high proportion of the effort associated with large projects is dedicated to administration.

On very large projects, there is always a danger that project staff cannot separate the wheat from the chaff as they are bombarded with project information. This ability becomes especially crucial in respect to tracking budgets and schedules. Given the plethora of data that are spewed out of the project planning and tracking machine, how can project staff make sense of the barrage of project performance facts and figures directed at them? Increasingly, they are turning to an approach called the *earned value technique* to help them better manage budget and schedule information.

The Earned Value Technique

The earned value technique was developed by cost accountants and is designed to help project staff keep better track of what is happening on their projects. It recognizes that cost data alone—or schedule data alone—can lead to distorted perceptions of performance. In Chapter Seven, we saw that this problem can be handled by viewing Gantt charts, cumulative cost curves, and resource loading charts together, a combination that provides us with an instant overview of schedule, budget, and resource performance. However, applying this approach to very large projects, with their tens of thousands of activities, would overwhelm project staff. For example, Gantt charts would be so massive and busy that it would be difficult to understand what they are saying.

The earned value approach does numerically what the graphical approach in Figure 7.9 does through charts. It allows project managers to examine cost and schedule variances concurrently, enabling them to take a holistic view of progress on the project. A number of high-level government program managers have told me that it is hard to imagine how very large projects could be controlled without this approach. In the U.S. government, incidentally, the earned value approach is given various names, including DODI (Department of Defense Instruction) 7000.2, the Cost/Schedule Control System Criteria, C/SCSC, (CS)-Squared, and C-Specs. The Department of Defense, the Department of Energy, and NASA require that contractors use this approach on very large projects.

The earned value technique is based on three fundamental building blocks. One is called the *budgeted cost of work scheduled* (BCWS). This is equivalent to the conventional concept of planned budget—that is, BCWS states what we think a particular task (or subtask or work package) will cost. A second building block is called the *actual cost of work performed* (ACWP). This is equivalent to the conventional concept of actual costs—that is, ACWP states how much we actually spent to accomplish a given effort.

So far, there is nothing new here. Project staff regularly use planned costs and actual costs to calculate cost variance. The earned value technique becomes interesting with the introduction of the concept of *budgeted cost of work performed* (BCWP), also known as *earned value.* A moment's reflection on the term *budgeted cost of work performed* offers an insight into BCWP's purpose. The "budgeted cost" component of this term means that we are concerned with our original *plan*, whereas the "work performed" component refers to what has *actually* been accomplished. Thus, BCWP—or earned value—is a hybrid measure, combining elements of the plan with elements of the actuals. With BCWP, we are evaluating our actual performance in terms of what we originally planned to accomplish.

An example will help to clarify the meaning of BCWP. Let us assume that, at the outset of a project, we estimate that task T will cost $1,000 to carry out and that it will be completed by November 1. However, on November 1, a review of progress on the task shows that it is only 70 percent complete. Although we have planned to undertake $1,000 worth of work (BCWS), we have actually achieved only $700 worth of work (BCWP). BCWP is a measure, then, of the dollar value of the work we have actually accomplished (hence the term *earned value*).

These three building blocks—BCWS, ACWP, and BCWP—allow us to calculate budget and schedule variance in a new, powerful way. Budget variance and schedule variance are each captured in a single number. These two numbers, when encountered concurrently, allow us to determine where we stand on our project from the perspective of both budget and schedule.

Budget variance is defined in the earned value approach as BCWP minus ACWP. To understand why, let's extend the example above to include information on actual cost of work performed, $500. BCWP tells us that we have done $700 worth of work, and ACWP tells us that it has cost us $500 to do so. Clearly, we are $200 (BCWP minus ACWP) ahead of the game for that portion of the work we have carried out. That is, we have a positive budget variance of $200. Does this mean we are in good shape? We cannot answer this question until we have examined schedule information.

In the earned value approach, schedule variance is defined as BCWP minus BCWS. Note that *schedule variance is here being interpreted in monetary terms!* We are looking at the difference between the work we planned to do and what we have actually done, valued according to our original budget estimates. Let's look at our example again to clarify the concept of schedule variance. We stated above that we planned to spend $1,000 on task T, but as of November 1 we have only done $700 worth of work (that is, our earned value is $700). The definition of schedule variance suggests that the dollar value of our schedule slippage is – $300 ($700 – $1,000). That is, we have yet to complete $300 worth of work that we were supposed to have completed.

Considering both budget and schedule variances together, we find ourselves in the following situation: We have slipped our schedule; although the task should have been completed by November 1, we find on that date that $300 worth of work remains to be carried out. Looking at the work we have completed

($700 worth), we find that it has cost us only $500 to undertake this work, suggesting a cost savings to date of $200. However, this savings is to a certain extent chimerical, because our schedule has slipped substantially. Had we dedicated more resources to the task, perhaps we could have avoided the schedule slippage.

The perceptive reader will have noted a fundamental weakness in the earned value technique. In order to calculate BCWP, it is necessary to know what percent of a task has been completed. If a task has not yet begun, we have no trouble saying that 0 percent of the task has been completed; and if the task is finished, it is obviously 100 percent completed. However, we walk on treacherous ground when we try to estimate how much of a task has been completed for anything between those two extremes. To see the nature of the difficulty, consider Imhotep's problem in determining how much work he had completed on a pyramid that had used 900,000 stone blocks out of a total of 1 million needed to complete the project. Looking at these statistics, we are tempted to say that 90 percent of the work has been completed, since 90 percent of the principal construction material has been utilized. The problem here is that the last 100,000 stone blocks have to be hauled higher than the first 900,000; furthermore, they have to be fitted into a point at the very top—a formidable task. Clearly, the pyramid project is somewhat less than 90 percent completed. If it is difficult to say how much of a project has been completed when we are dealing with a down-to-earth, tangible undertaking, consider the added difficulty of making such estimates on information-age projects that operate largely in the realm of the intangible.

The earned value approach has a means of dealing with this problem: the 50-50 rule. Project staff are not asked to make wild estimates of how much of their task has been completed. Rather, as soon as a task is begun, it is assumed that half the effort has been completed, and half of the BCWS value associated with the task is entered into the project accounts book. Only after the task is completed is the remaining half of the BCWS value entered into the accounts. When there are many tasks being considered, this approach provides a good statistical approximation of BCWP. In Figure 8.1, the pictured Gantt chart shows five tasks, each of which represents $100 worth of work. Four of the five tasks have been begun; three of those four have been completed (leaving one partially completed task and one task not yet begun). Using the 50-50 approach, we enter into our accounts that we have completed $300 worth of effort with the three finished tasks, and we enter another $50 to take into account the task that has been begun but is not yet finished. Inasmuch as we have not yet begun the fifth task, we enter nothing into the accounts for this task. What is earned value? Answer: $350. BCWS for the five tasks is, of course, $500, and we can now use this figure to calculate schedule slippage. That is, we have completed $350 worth of work, but we should have

Figure 8.1. Application of the 50-50 Rule.

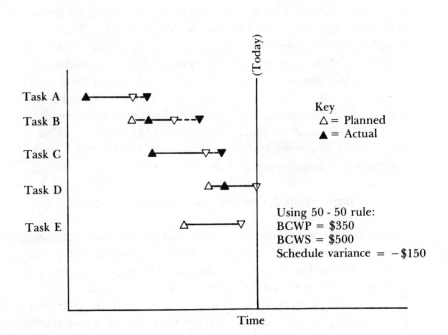

Key
△ = Planned
▲ = Actual

Using 50 - 50 rule:
BCWP = $350
BCWS = $500
Schedule variance = −$150

Time

completed $500 worth of work; so our schedule has slipped to the tune of $150 worth of work. These data also enable us to calculate that we have completed only 70 percent (that is, $350/500 \times 100$) of the work scheduled on the five tasks.

Of those individuals who prefer a more conservative approach than the 50-50 rule, many adopt a 10-90 rule. As soon as a task is begun, 10 percent of its value is entered into the project accounts. As soon as it is completed, the remaining 90 percent of its value is entered. Using this conservative rule to calculate BCWP, we find that BCWP on our above example is now $310. This suggests that we are only 62 percent (that is, $310/500 \times 100$) finished with the five tasks.

Many project management experts strongly believe that the earned value approach is vital for the control of very large projects. I would like to offer that it can be useful on small projects as well. On very large federal projects, the rules for implementing Department of Defense Instruction 7000.2 are very complex; for example, they require major contractors to overhaul completely their cost-accounting systems to accommodate the earned value approach. However, on small projects, there is no need to follow the complex rules. All one needs in order to implement the earned value system are estimates of planned task costs (BCWS), data on actual expenditures (ACWP), and a good guess on the percentage of work completed on the task (a risky approach) or employment of the 50-50 rule.

Planning and Control for Multiple Projects

Projects are often organized into a portfolio, *a collection of projects that must be co-managed*. Whether these projects are interrelated or independent of each other, the important thing is that they fall under a single management umbrella.

Project portfolios are found in many different situations. For example, they are common in data processing departments, where staff are busily working on a wide array of projects—some long-term, some short-term, some large, some small. Management consultant firms often are nothing more—from a functional perspective—than a conglomeration of individual projects. Similarly, multiple projects are the rule in R & D departments, auditing departments, and advertising agencies.

The Project Portfolio

Project portfolios come in many different shapes and sizes. Figure 8.2 shows three different forms that portfolios can assume. The structural relations embedded in each of these forms present managers with different challenges and requirements. Figure 8.2a pictures a portfolio of projects that deal with the same basic subject matter but are otherwise independent of each other; the outcome of one project has little or no bearing on work on the other projects. Research projects in an electronics laboratory have this characteristic. What ties the projects together is a strong project selection process, which filters out project possibilities that have nothing to do with, say, the mission of the electronics laboratory. The principal management challenge associated with this kind of portfolio is selection of appropriate projects. Because the projects are independent, the matter of coordinating their activities does not loom large. Planning and control issues are primarily the responsibility of the individual project managers.

In Figure 8.2b, the portfolio constitutes what is often referred to as a *program* (for example, the Apollo program, the space shuttle program). Its chief characteristic is the heavy interdependence of projects that comprise the portfolio. These assorted projects dovetail tightly and are directed toward a common outcome. If a project runs into trouble, the whole portfolio may be jeopardized. Consequently, this kind of portfolio requires vigilant portfolio-wide planning and control efforts. Typically, a program office is set up to carry out these efforts, and a powerful program manager holds sway over the entire portfolio.

Figure 8.2c portrays a portfolio that is nothing more than a loose agglomeration of projects with little or nothing in common. Planning and control here are the responsibility of the individual project managers.

Figure 8.2. Varieties of Project Portfolios.

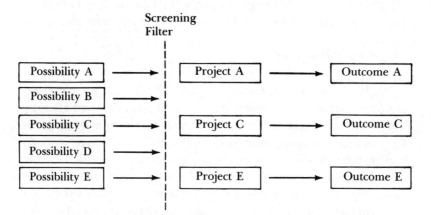

8.2a.   Portfolio of Independent Projects That Have Much in Common.

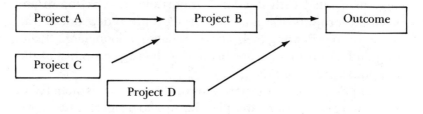

8.2b.   Portfolio of Interdependent Projects (a Program).

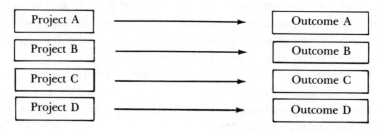

8.2c.   Portfolio of Independent Projects.

Special Considerations in Managing a Portfolio. There is usually more complexity involved in the management of a portfolio of projects than of a single project. Let's look at some of the reasons.

• *Portfolios are administratively more complex than single projects.* To see this, one need merely consider the differences in managing a single $1 million project versus ten $100,000 projects. While the $1 million project has one project manager, the portfolio of smaller projects will have several managers. With the $1 million project, there is only one project to plan and track; with the smaller projects in a portfolio, there are ten projects that must be followed. In general, the ten smaller projects will collectively have more administrative overhead associated with them—more forms to be filled out, more project review meetings—than will the one larger project.

• *Optimization of the portfolio's performance will require suboptimization of individual projects.* The portfolio manager's objective is to optimize portfolio performance, and this invariably requires him or her to make resource allocation and scheduling decisions that benefit high-priority projects at the expense of low-priority projects. While suboptimization of individual projects may be necessary to enhance the good of the portfolio, this is small consolation to the manager of the suboptimized project, whose credo is "Get the job done—on time, within budget, and according to specifications!" Consequently, portfolio managers are likely to face unhappiness and resistance from some quarters of their portfolio staff.

• *Portfolios run the risk of falling victim to the tyranny of large projects.* It is difficult to maintain a balanced perspective on large and small projects that may coexist in a portfolio. Large projects, by definition, have a more pronounced profile than small projects; they are more visible. They tend to have access to the best of scarce resources. Furthermore, when large projects run into trouble, small projects in the portfolio often get lost in the shuffle. Their meager resources may even be diverted away from them and directed toward the large projects. When that occurs, we find not only the large projects in trouble but the small ones as well.

Sequencing Projects in the Portfolio. How projects are sequenced in the portfolio may have a strong bearing on the portfolio's performance. For example, in a program of heavily interrelated projects, considerable planning may be required to identify start and finish dates of projects that will enhance program performance. If these dates have not been carefully chosen, scheduling bottlenecks may arise and the overall program performance may deteriorate.

The way in which projects are sequenced in the portfolio also has an impact on the flow of benefits emerging from them (for example, profits, units of output produced, increased productivity). In Figure 8.3a, projects A and B—which have equal budgets—are carried out concurrently. Benefits do not emerge from them until both are finished. In Figure 8.3b, the budgets for projects A and B are the same size as in Figure 8.3a, and the budget period covered is of the same duration. However, the benefit streams emerging from the projects are quite different. Benefits begin earlier here, emerging just as soon as A is completed. For the time period shown in the figure, the benefit stream for A is larger in the second case, while the benefit stream for B is equal in both cases. Consequently, from the perspective of benefit streams, the second scenario—picturing projects carried out one after the other—is better.

Gap Analysis

Chapter Seven discussed the difficulties in producing a budget for a single project. Budget allocations for a portfolio of multiple projects present even greater challenges. With a portfolio, we typically face the situation our grandmothers encountered when they had to divide up an apple pie among a throng of grandchildren of different shapes and sizes—that is, we have a fixed budget to work with, and there are obvious practical limits on how we can carve it up. We may opt to spread our funds over many small projects, or we may decide to concentrate them on one or two larger efforts, or we may take some position between these two extremes.

Figure 8.3. Project Scheduling Sequences Affect Output Flows.

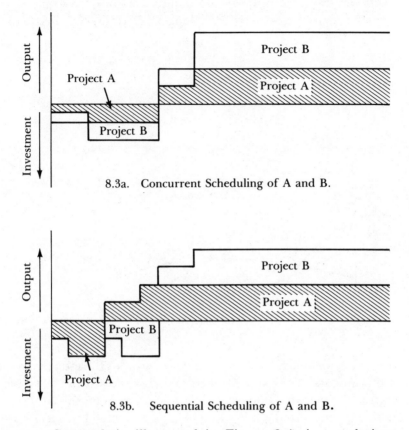

8.3a.   Concurrent Scheduling of A and B.

8.3b.   Sequential Scheduling of A and B.

Gap analysis, illustrated in Figure 8.4, is a technique that can be helpful in allowing project managers to visualize the practical budget options available to them in project portfolios. Gap analysis employs both exploratory and normative forecasting. It uses exploratory forecasting when it requires us to make estimates of the future budget demands of projects that are currently in our portfolio. In Figure 8.4, we have these estimates for projects A, B, C, and D. Note that these budget curves are a pictorial representation of the anticipated project life cycle for each of the four projects. After future budgets for individual projects have been made, these budgets are added together to create a total budget for projects currently in the portfolio. Because projects ultimately are completed and no longer consume resources, the long-term trend for this total budget is downward.

Figure 8.4. Gap Analysis.

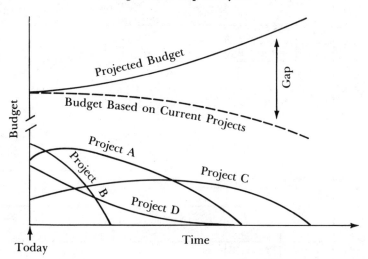

In gap analysis, the curve associated with the total budget requirements of existing projects is compared with a curve of the total anticipated budget for *all* projects, even those that have not yet been started. In Figure 8.4, this projected budget is rising, while the budget for existing projects is declining, leaving an ever-growing gap between the two over time. It is at this point that normative forecasting enters the picture. We examine the anticipated gap and then ask ourselves, "What should the project portfolio look like in order to fill the gap?" At one extreme, we could try to fill the gap by initiating a single large project; its budget would take up the slack created by the winding down of existing projects. At the other extreme, we could plan to increase the number of projects in the portfolio by carrying out more and more small projects. Gap analysis does not provide an automatic answer to this question of how portfolios should be constructed, but it can serve as a useful tool that helps planners conceptualize the future character of their portfolios.

Planning and Control for Contracted Projects

A large number of projects are carried out under contractual arrangements. Construction projects, for example, are often based on a contractual agreement between a developer, who organizes project financing, and a contractor, who oversees the actual construction effort. The contractor, in turn, works with subcontractors, each of whom specializes in a particular area, such as plumbing, electrical wiring, heating-ventilation, and carpentry.

The largest funder of project contracts is, of course, government. The federal government issues billions of dollars of contracts each year for projects ranging from the minor modification of software all the way up to the building of a space defense system. Similarly, state and local governments carry out most of the project work they need done through contractors. Everything from establishing an alcohol inventory system for the state liquor control board to redesigning a science curriculum for a municipal school system is fair game for contracts.

Contracted projects are also common in the private sector, where big and little companies alike employ outside expertise to help them address special needs that cannot be handled cost-effectively with internal resources. A huge industry has emerged whose principal function is to service the needs of companies and government by carrying out specialized project work through contracts—exemplified by the likes of research firms such as Arthur Andersen & Co., Arthur D. Little, Inc., and Arthur Young & Co.

When we talk about project management in contracted projects, we add another layer of complexity to an already complex situation. The end-users are now outside the performing organization. Those end-users, who are paying hard-earned cash for results, are going to be very interested in getting their money's worth out of the project. Consequently, they may insist on playing an overactive role in overseeing progress on the project and may, in fact, perceive themselves to be de facto project managers, the individuals calling the shots. Furthermore, the questions discussed in Chapters Five and Six on meeting end-users' needs and specifying project requirements take on an added urgency with contracted projects, since unhappy end-users may now mean costly and painful litigation.

Types of Contracts

A contract is a legally binding agreement specifying the rights and responsibilities of the contracting parties. Contracts can assume an endless variety of forms. Common contract forms found in project situations include the following:

- firm fixed-price
- fixed-price, economic price adjustment
- fixed-price, incentive
- fixed-price, award
- fixed-price, with provisions for redetermination
- firm fixed-price, level of effort term
- cost
- cost sharing
- cost plus incentive
- cost plus award fee
- cost plus fixed fee
- time and materials

To understand the impact of contractual arrangement on the management of projects, we need not delve into the intricacies of all the different kinds of contracts that exist. Rather, we will focus on the two most common types of contracted projects: fixed-price and cost-plus.

Fixed-Price Contracts. With a fixed-price contract, funder and performer negotiate a price for undertaking the project. The performer agrees to do what is described in the contract for a flat price. If the performer can carry out project work at a cost below the price, he or she will realize a profit. If it costs more to undertake the project than the negotiated contract price, the performer faces a loss.

With fixed-price contracts, project managers in performing organizations face enormous pressures to reduce project costs, because every cent saved is translated into an increase in profit margins. Many project organizations that regularly carry out fixed-price contracts offer incentives to their project managers to keep costs down. For example, project managers may be given bonuses whose value is tied to decreases in project costs from the original plan. On the surface, this may seem to be a worthy tactic that rewards project managers who can effectively promote efficiency on their projects. However, there is a danger that corner cutting is being encouraged and that cost savings will be realized at the expense of quality.

Theoretically, fixed-price contracts place project management responsibilities totally in the hands of the performer, since the performer has agreed to do certain things for a given price. If it costs him or her more—well, that's the performer's problem. Theoretically, all the funder has to do is sit back and wait for the results to be delivered on the promised date. In practice, the funder must maintain vigilance in observing the performer's work. A fixed-price contract is an agreement, not a guarantee that the deliverable will be turned over on time and as promised. Things have a way of turning out differently than anticipated. A delay may arise in shipping the deliverable, and this could seriously hurt the funder. A dispute may flare up as to whether the deliverable is what the funder ordered, or whether the quality of the deliverable is acceptable. The unhappy funder can wave the fixed-price contract under the nose of the performer, but this contract reminder offers no assurance that the funder's desires will be satisfied. As a last resort, the funder can take the performer to court—a costly and painful procedure that may or may not work out to the advantage of the funder.

From the perspective of the project manager working in the performing organization, fixed-price projects can be stressful, especially when things start going wrong. If costs get out of hand, profits shrink; in the worst case scenario, the project actually generates losses for the performing organization. Experienced performing organizations typically shy away from entering into fixed-price arrangements on unpredictable, nonroutine projects. If they do undertake a risky fixed-price project, they charge a high-risk premium, generously inflating estimates of project costs to account for unanticipated contingencies.

Cost-Plus Contracts. With a cost-plus contract, the funder agrees to reimburse the performer for project work and offers an additional fee or bonus, so that the performing organization can earn a profit on its efforts. These contracts are common on highly speculative projects—projects on which it is difficult or impossible to predict accurately what the project will cost.

Project managers in the performing organization face far fewer pressures on cost-plus contracts than on fixed-price contracts. If there are cost overruns, the additional cost is borne by the funder, not the performer. There is always a danger on cost-plus contracts that the performer will grow lax in monitoring progress. With poorly monitored cost-plus contracts, it is easy for spending to get out of hand, since there are no obvious penalties for profligacy. There may even be incentives for overspending, because spending creates work for staff who might otherwise be idle. Ultimately, profligacy can backfire, particularly if the performer develops a reputation for being a big-time spender.

Given the lack of obvious cost restraints facing the performer, the funder must actively monitor project efforts on cost-plus contracts. The performer may be required to submit twice-monthly progress reports to the funder, for example, and to present monthly briefings. On significant projects, the funder may insist on having a company representative working on-site in the performing organization, in order to monitor project efforts continuously. Although it is crucial that the funding organization keep track of project developments, it should avoid meddling to the point that it contributes to project failure.

Managing Changes to the Plan on Contracted Projects

As I have mentioned several times, project managers can count on changes to the project plan. With contracted fixed-price projects, project managers in the performing organization must consciously employ an explicit methodology for dealing with change requests from the funder, since, more often than not, changes increase project costs. Building contractors are sensitive about this point and demand that their staff keep track of all changes requested by the funder—no matter how small—so that the funder can be billed for the changes. In the absence of such a policy, fragile profit margins can disappear quickly.

Without an explicit policy for dealing with change requests, naive project managers can get into serious trouble. In their eagerness to please the client, they may acquiesce to nickel-and-dime changes here and there. After a while, they realize that the nickels and dimes are adding up and putting a squeeze on profit margins. At this point, it is difficult to know what to do, because they have already established a pattern of compliance with end-user requests. They worry that any reluctance to meet end-user requests will be perceived as a sign of unresponsiveness to end-user needs. Yet they also recognize that they cannot go on "eating" the extra costs resulting from the changes to the project.

It is far better for project performers to make it clear to funders at the outset that any funder-requested changes to the plan will be noted and that the funder will be responsible for their cost. Each time that funders want a change, they should be required to fill out a change order. Before the change is actually implemented, the funder should be told what the cost of the request will be. If the funder still wants to go ahead with the change, he or she should be asked to sign a statement to this effect, so that it is perfectly clear that the funder recognizes the cost consequences of his or her request. This policy will force the funder to think twice before requesting changes. It will also avoid putting the performing organization's project manager in a position of switching from compliance with to hard-nosed resistance to end-user requests. (Change orders are discussed in more detail in Chapter Six.)

Government Versus Private Sector Contracted Projects

Several years ago, I did some work with a company that had recently established a Washington, D.C., operation. The company's Washington strategy was to grow 30 percent per year, with all new business taking the form of federal contracts. I met with over eighty corporate project managers, the majority of whom had been transferred to the new Washington facility from corporate headquarters out West. Most of these project managers were unhappy with their Washington contracts and were sour on doing business with government. They longed to return to private sector work. This feeling was so common among the project managers that I decided to investigate the sources of unhappiness. I invited the project managers to describe to me their perceptions of government work, and to contrast this with work in the private sector. The responses, quite uniform, boiled down to a handful of points.

Two points in particular stand out. First, there was a general perception that it is difficult to do business with government because government is slow and bureaucratic. A contract that may take a few days to work out in the private sector will likely take months or years to negotiate in the government sector. Second, there was a sense that the government wants something for nothing in dealing with the contractor. This is particularly evident in fixed-price contracts, they claimed: government end-users may request changes to the project and then, after the changes have been made, refuse to authorize payment for the changes (since they were not covered in the original contract).

Virtually all of the project managers believed that doing business with the private sector was more satisfying. They noted that in the private sector there is an emphasis on good faith and flexibility. All parties recognize that it is in everyone's best interest to get the job done as effectively as possible. If the contractor does not perform satisfactorily, he or she will not get repeat business. (As the national news accounts attest, the situation is different with government: poor performance and corruption are no barrier to obtaining government work for the large government contractor!) If modifications to the project are requested, the requests are sealed with a handshake, and the funder recognizes that the contractor should not be expected to eat the additional costs incurred by the modification.

Of course, when asked their opinion about contractor performance on projects, *government* project officers held a different view. For the most part, they agreed that the government contracting procedure is cumbersome and difficult to deal with. However, they pointed out that there is ample evidence to show that many contractors take advantage of the government whenever they can, and plenty of major scandals attest to this fact. They also suggested that, because government is so large, strong budget control procedures must be implemented on projects. For example, in order to avoid requests for costly changes on projects by overenthusiastic government end-users, only contract officers are authorized to approve change orders. Without such tight control, there would be few constraints keeping end-users in line.

In general, government-funded contracted projects are more difficult to manage than corresponding private sector projects. This is primarily a consequence of the fact that large pieces of the project management process are governed not by good sense but by rules and regulations that, in the context of a given project, may be arbitrary and unwise. An important key to minimizing problems in government projects is knowledge of the legal and administrative aspects of the contracting procedure. This is important for both the contractor and the government funder. To the extent that each side knows what is allowable under certain circumstances, many of the problems rampant in government contracted projects can be dramatically reduced.

Planning and Control with Bureaucratic Milestones

Project management instructional material typically focuses on schedule optimization or resource optimization. Yet in many bureaucratic organizations, successful planning has less to do with schedule or resource optimization than with identifying key bureaucratic milestones of importance to the organization, and sequencing tasks in such a way that the milestones are achieved. These milestones are often tied to the organization's budget cycle. For example, all project managers desiring funding in the fiscal 1992 budget may be required to have preliminary budget requests filed by December 1990. Frequently these milestones are unforgiving: if you miss the December 1990 filing date, your project may not get funded in fiscal 1992. Given this bureaucratic reality found in many organizations, it would seem a wise policy for project staff to plan their projects around such milestones.

Technical people often pay little attention to bureaucratic milestones. They resent having their work governed by arbitrary requirements that have no logical bearing on their projects. Typically, they simply ignore the milestones or put off meeting the requirements of the milestones until the last possible moment. While the resentment of arbitrary milestones is understandable, resisting or ignoring them is often dangerous. By the same token, as we saw in Chapter Two, project staff who become masters of bureaucratic intricacies can use their skills to develop bureaucratic authority that will help them negotiate their projects through the inscrutable maze of the bureaucracy.

Figure 8.5 pictures a planning and control tool developed a few years ago by a number of Navy project managers. These project managers looked around their organization and saw projects failing right and left. They analyzed these failures and determined the number one cause of failure to be inattention to arbitrary, organizationally imposed milestone requirements. Project managers did not have budget requests, or progress reports, or test data submitted at bureaucratically crucial times; as a consequence, they often lost their funding.

The planning and control tool that they developed, the milestone review technique, consists of three tiers: organizational, project management, and performer. The top tier notes the crucial organizationally imposed milestones. In order to keep Figure 8.5 simple, only one milestone is portrayed—a requirement to submit a preliminary project budget request in December. In practice, there would be many milestones noted at this level.

The next level down represents the special requirements that project managers must concentrate on in order to address the organizationally imposed milestones. For example, as Figure 8.5 shows, management must review the technical and financial

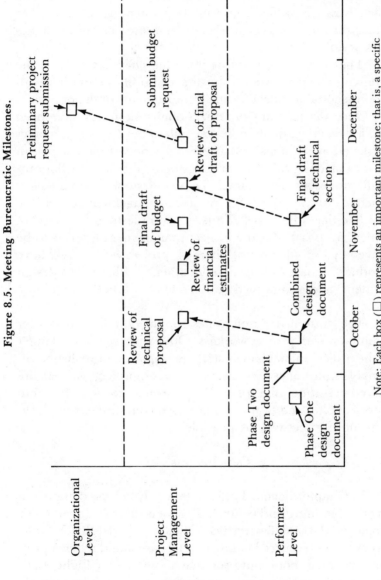

Figure 8.5. Meeting Bureaucratic Milestones.

Note: Each box (□) represents an important milestone; that is, a specific point in time when a task or series of tasks (not pictured here) is scheduled to be completed.

elements of the project that will be incorporated into the final draft of the budget request.

The bottom level represents milestones that project workers must achieve if the December budget request deadline is to be achieved. Much of the project manager's energy is devoted to making sure that project workers take these bottom-tier milestones seriously.

The construction of this planning chart starts from the top down. The first order of business is to fill the top tier with the nonnegotiable "drop dead" requirements of the organization. Once the relevant organizational milestones have been noted for this tier, the middle-tier milestones (project management level) are established. These milestones are created with a view to meeting the top-tier milestones. Finally, the bottom-tier milestones are determined. These milestones are sequenced in such a way as to enable project management to achieve its middle-tier milestones. Thus, if the milestone "Review of technical proposal" (at the project management level) is to be achieved by mid-October as planned, project workers will have to produce a Phase One design document, a Phase Two design document, and a combined design document on the appointed dates.

The bottom-tier milestones should be established after consultation with project workers. Otherwise, there is a danger that the project management staff are imposing unrealistic, unattainable milestones. Furthermore, when project workers are involved in setting milestones, they are encouraged to buy into the project plan and to make a personal commitment to carrying it out as effectively as possible.

Conclusions

In Chapter Seven, I offer a generally accepted approach to project planning and control. The tools discussed there—for example, work-breakdown structures, Gantt charts, PERT/CPM networks, and resource loading charts—are found in most project management books and seminars. In Chapter Eight, I address a number of planning and control topics that many project managers face but that are not as widely discussed.

I hope that the emphasis on tools in these two chapters does not obscure the important lesson that successful planning and control is more a function of attitude and commitment than the routine application of tools. A project whose team spends a good deal of time developing a thoughtful qualitative plan that team members agree is viable has a higher likelihood of success than a project where plans are developed by one or two people working alone with a sophisticated, computer-driven PERT/CPM network. Similarly, an attitude reflecting the view "I've just got to keep on top of project developments" is far more important for project control than the routine generation of monthly progress reports.

Of course, it should not be an either/or proposition. The combination of strong commitment and good tools is the best possible situation, reducing dramatically the likelihood of all-too-frequent project failure caused by planning and control deficiencies.

 9

Achieving Results:
The Key to Success
as a Project Manager

One common problem project managers face is getting so caught up in the helter-skelter of putting out fires, focusing on minutiae, that they lose the big-picture perspective. When things are popping all around them, it is difficult for them to step back and view their projects from a distance. In this last chapter, we do precisely that—stand back and take a big-picture view of the project management process as it pertains to information-age projects. After all is said and done, what are the elements of good project management—the most rudimentary principles—that we should keep in mind in order to maximize the likelihood that we will bring our project to a successful conclusion?

Rudimentary Principles

There are five basic principles that, if followed, will help project managers immeasurably in their efforts. I will discuss each in turn.

- Be conscious of what you are doing; don't be an accidental manager.

- Invest heavily in the front-end spadework; get it right the first time.
- Anticipate the problems that will inevitably arise.
- Go beneath surface illusions; dig deeply to find the real situation.
- Be as flexible as possible; don't get sucked into unnecessary rigidity and formality.

Be conscious of what you are doing; don't be an accidental manager. In the Preface it was noted that project management has been called the accidental profession. Men and women stumble into project management responsibilities accidentally, only vaguely aware of what projects are and how they should be managed. Their management approach is pure trial and error. They reinvent the wheel, and in most cases do a bad job of it. The pity is that much of the grief they encounter and much of the waste they engender could be avoided if they simply made an effort to learn something about the theory and practice of project management. For example, if they learned that project staff are usually borrowed workers over whom the great majority of project managers have no direct control, they could direct their energies toward *influencing* these workers to do well rather than spend time sulking in a corner because of the workers' perceived insubordination and lack of commitment.

In order to maintain consciousness of the fact that they are working on something over which they have the power to do a good job—*if only they knew what they were doing*—perhaps project managers should say to themselves several times a day, "I am a project manager. I work on projects. Projects are undertakings that are goal-oriented, complex, finite, and unique. They pass through a life cycle, which begins with project selection and ends with project termination." The purpose of this ritualistic litany is simply to remind the project manager that over the past several decades many people have thought a lot about what projects are and what their management entails. Projects are hard to manage even when we know what we are doing. They are nearly impossible to manage by accident and happenstance.

Invest heavily in the front-end spadework; get it right the first time.
Many of us have a tendency to rush in where angels fear to tread.
We tend to leap before we look. We are results-oriented and,
given our fixation on results, often overlook some rudimentary
matters regarding the basic steps it takes to achieve these results.
This characteristic serves some people well: by throwing cau-
tion to the wind, they achieve breakthroughs that more cautious
people would never accomplish. Such people are trailblazers—
bold, dynamic, and filled with exuberant energy.

This tendency to leap before we look also has its drawbacks. Where, for example, does one draw the line separating
boldness from impetuosity? Fearlessness from foolishness? In
many situations, a moment's reflection on what action to pursue is more important than boldness. For the most part, projects can use more forethought and less impetuosity. By definition, projects are unique, goal-oriented systems; consequently,
they are complex. Because they are complex, they cannot be
managed effectively in an offhand, ad hoc fashion. They must
be carefully selected and carefully planned. A good deal of
thought must be directed at determining how they should be
structured. Great amounts of time must be spent hand holding
with end-users to assure that the final deliverable is something
they find useful.

Care taken at the outset of a project to do things right
will generally pay for itself handsomely. Doing things right takes
time and effort. For example, it takes time to find out what the
real needs are on a project, to specify requirements carefully,
and to plan out a course of action for accomplishing project objectives. For impetuous people, it is far more satisfying to rush
into projects and begin solving problems than to identify precisely what those problems are. Unfortunately, if the proper
spadework is not done at the outset of a project, it is likely that
various project tasks will not be done properly; those tasks will
have to be redone again and again until project staff finally get
them right. Rework, however, is expensive. It is invariably more
expensive to do something over again than to take the time to
do it right at the outset.

Anticipate the problems that will inevitably arise. One thing this book has stressed repeatedly is that many of the problems faced by project managers are predictable. For example, if project managers are working in a matrix organization, we know that they will face the following people problems:

- They will have little or no direct control over the borrowed staff members.
- Their staff will have little commitment to the project.
- Their staff are not likely to be precisely the workers they want or need.

We can also count on the following additional realities:

- The goals of portfolio managers are often different from those of individual project managers, since maximization of portfolio performance will likely require suboptimization of the performance of individual projects.
- Schedule and budget variances will occur, since it is impossible to predict the future precisely; so we should not ask, "Do we have variances?" but rather, "Are the variances we face acceptable?"
- End-user needs will shift.
- If project requirements are stated vaguely, they are likely to be misinterpreted. (They may be misinterpreted even when they are stated precisely!)
- Overplanning and overcontrol will lead to project inefficiencies and may result in cost and schedule overruns, just as underplanning and weak control may lead to cost and schedule overruns.
- All projects have a hidden agenda, which is usually far more important than the stated agenda.

By reviewing these inevitable realities (and this is only a small sampling from a much larger list), we see that conflict and problems are built into projects—*they are going to arise!* If we anticipate these problems, however, we can determine ahead of time how to cope with them; as we become more experienced project managers, we can even learn how to use them to our advantage.

Go beneath surface illusions; dig deeply to find the real situation. Project managers are continually getting into trouble because they accept things at face value. For example, end-users usually have only the vaguest conception of what their needs are, even when they think they know *exactly* what they want. The project manager who blindly accepts the end-user's needs statement is likely to encounter end-user requests later on for major changes in the project; or perhaps that manager will produce a deliverable that the end-user rejects, saying, "This is neither what I asked for nor what I want." Another example: A project manager, assuming that secretaries are the end-users of a project to install word processors in the office, fails to determine the needs of such hidden end-users as the secretaries' bosses, the office's clients, and the division's information resource manager. Consequently, while secretaries' needs are met, the needs of the other significant actors may be unsatisfied, possibly resulting in project failure. To the extent that project managers do not understand what is really happening on their projects, they are likely to be chasing after shadows. They will not make the right decisions.

Robert Block's approach to project politics—described in *The Politics of Projects* (Block, 1983)—can greatly help project managers to be more realistic. Using his approach, project managers systematically go through a number of steps designed to let them penetrate surface illusions and identify what is really happening. First they identify all the players, paying special attention to those players who can have an impact on the project outcome. Then they try to determine the goals of the players and the organization, focusing particularly on hidden goals. Having done this, they assess their own strengths and weaknesses. It is only at this point that they should begin defining the problems facing them in their project. It is crucial to the problem-definition step that project managers root their efforts in reality—isolating the facts, identifying the real situation, and recognizing the assumptions underlying the whole project effort.

Once the problem is defined adequately, they can develop solutions, test them, and fine-tune them. (See Chapter Two for a more complete discussion of Block's approach.)

Be as flexible as possible; don't get sucked into unnecessary rigidity and formality. Project management can be viewed as a struggle against the basic principle of the second law of thermodynamics, which states that things tend to dissolve into a state of random disorder. With project management, we try to reverse this sequence; we strive to create order where the natural state of things seems to be chaos. In our drive to create order, however, we run the risk of sacrificing reasonable flexibility on the altar of formal project requirements. The rationale for inflexibility is that order comes from structure: we convince ourselves that the more formal the structure we impose on our projects, the less chaos we face. Thus, we may require all project changes to be approved by three levels of management, and we may require staff to fill out six-page progress reports every week. We may also put together very detailed plans for our project, so that nothing is left to chance. We may hold daily staff meetings to make sure that workers know what they are supposed to do. And so on. In our attempt to realize order, we may instead achieve stifling bureaucracy.

One of the hardest tasks facing policy makers in project organizations is striking a balance between the need for order and the contrary need for flexibility. Why is flexibility necessary? Because projects are full of surprises, and overly rigid systems cannot respond adequately to surprises, just as a rigid stick will snap after it has been bent only a little. This is especially true with information-age projects, which deal with intangibles and tend to be amorphous. By their very nature, they are hard to plan in detail and they defy attempts at tight controls.

Too often people do not understand that order can be attained without excessive formality. If we are conscious of what we are doing on projects and avoid being accidental project managers, if we invest in front-end spadework, if we anticipate inevitable problems, and if we penetrate beneath surface illusions, we will help establish order in our projects. If, in addition, we reject unnecessary formality and rigidity, we may be able to have our cake and eat it too—that is, we may be able to achieve order and flexibility simultaneously.

Strong degrees of formality are appropriate on some projects. For example, as projects get larger, the number of communication channels that must be maintained grows explosively, and formal protocols must be established to coordinate communication efforts. As a consequence, it is common in programs with budgets greater than $100 million to find from 50 to 65 percent of the total project budget dedicated to project administration. Heavy formality may also be appropriate on low-risk projects when we know precisely what must be done to produce the desired deliverable. When we build a house in a development of nearly identical houses, for example, we specify *in detail* many formal requirements that project staff should meet; we leave nothing to chance. Such low-risk projects have a minimal need for flexibility, since they encounter fewer surprises than high-risk projects.

Information-age projects typically do not fall into either of these two categories. First, because they deal more with information than with bricks and mortar, they do not usually achieve the size of projects to construct buildings or to build fighter aircraft. Second, because they deal with intangibles and are hard to get a handle, on, they tend to be filled with uncertainty. Given the smaller size of typical information-age projects, and their high degree of uncertainty, the need for rigid formality in their management is very low; therefore, in most such cases, formality is undesirable.

Last Word

As I stated in the first chapter, I envision this book as a travel guide. In part, it is a road map, showing readers the twists and turns, obstacles, and potholes they are likely to encounter on their journey into the realm of project management. In part, it is a repair guide, focusing primarily on preventive maintenance—avoiding breakdowns—but also offering instructions on fixing minor problems.

I suppose that my travel guide is a bit more cautionary in tone than the typical travel guide written for travelers to, say, the Greek Isles or Scotland. In these typical travel guides, the writers usually engage in extravagant hyperbole, extolling the beauties of the countryside and offering fascinating historical detail that makes readers wish fervently that they had lived in the region during its heyday. My travel guide is more like a guide to Beirut, Belfast, or Afghanistan in the late 1980s. While the guide to Scotland may spend most of its time addressing the best restaurants to visit, the variety of local flora and fauna, historical tidbits, and the like, the guide to Afghanistan focuses on avoidance of land mines, how to make and apply a tourniquet, and the fifty-seven different ways to camouflage oneself against helicopter attack in rocky terrain.

In my opinion, the project management environment is clearly more akin to the environment of Afghanistan than of Scotland. Wandering through project management terrain can be dangerous to the naive. In the land of project management, things can *and will* go awry.

Having said this, I want to add that being a project manager can be an enormously rewarding experience. For many individuals, managing projects is a first foray into the realm of management. It allows them to develop the management skills they need for career advancement. In addition, it offers them an independence of action and a degree of responsibility they infrequently encounter in other areas. For people who thrive on challenges, who like to solve problems creatively, and who enjoy creating order out of chaos, the management of projects can be exhilarating.

Selected Bibliography

Anderson, S. D. *Project Manpower Management*. New York: Wiley, 1981.

Archibald, R. D. *Managing High-Technology Programs and Projects*. New York: Wiley, 1976.

Augustine, N. R. *Augustine's Laws and Major System Development Programs*. Washington, D.C.: American Institute of Aeronautics and Astronautics, 1983.

Awani, A. O. *Project Management Techniques*. San Francisco: Petrocelli Books, 1983.

Bennigson, L. A. *Project Management*. Stockholm: Scandinavian Institutes for Administrative Research, 1977.

Bergland, G. D., and Gordon, R. D. *Software Design Strategies*. Los Angeles: IEEE Computer Society, 1982.

Blanchard, K., and Johnson, S. *The One Minute Manager*. New York: Morrow, 1982.

Block, R. *The Politics of Projects*. New York: Yourdon Press, 1983.

Boar, B. *Application Prototyping: A Requirements Definition Strategy for the 80s*. New York: Wiley, 1984.

Brill, A. E. (ed.). *Techniques of EDP Project Management*. New York: Yourdon Press, 1984.

Brooks, F. P. *The Mythical Man-Month: Essays on Software Engineering*. Reading, Mass.: Addison-Wesley, 1975.

Burman, P. J. *Precedence Networks for Project Planning and Control*. New York: McGraw-Hill, 1972.

Cleland, D. I., and King, W. R. (eds.). *Project Management Handbook*. New York: Van Nostrand Reinhold, 1983.

Cleland, D. I., and King, W. R. *Systems Analysis and Project Management*. New York: McGraw-Hill, 1983.

Clifton, D. S. *Project Feasibility Analysis*. New York: Wiley, 1975.

Clough, R. H. *Construction Project Management*. New York: Wiley, 1979.

Coutinho, J. de S. *Advanced Systems Development Management*. New York: Wiley, 1977.

Davies, C. *Organization for Program Management*. New York: Wiley, 1979.

DeMarco, T. *Controlling Software Projects*. New York: Yourdon Press, 1982.

Dinsmore, P. C. *Human Factors in Project Management*. New York: American Management Association, 1984.

Dyer, L. *Project Management*. Ithaca, N.Y.: Cornell University Press, 1976.

Gido, J. *An Introduction to Project Planning*. Schenectady, N.Y.: Project Planning Associates, 1984.

Hajek, V. G. *Management of Engineering Projects*. New York: McGraw-Hill, 1984.

Harrison, F. L. *Advanced Project Management*. New York: Wiley, 1984.

Hoare, H. R. *Project Management Using Network Analysis*. New York: McGraw-Hill, 1973.

Kendrick, D. A. *The Planning of Industrial Investment Programs*. Baltimore: Johns Hopkins University Press, 1978.

Kerzner, H. *Project Management for Bankers*. New York: Van Nostrand Reinhold, 1980.

Kerzner, H. *Project Management for Executives*. New York: Van Nostrand Reinhold, 1982.

Kerzner, H. *Project Management*. New York: Van Nostrand Reinhold, 1984.

Kerzner, H. *Project Management for Small and Medium Size Businesses*. New York: Van Nostrand Reinhold, 1984.

Kerzner, H. *Project/Matrix Management Policy and Strategy*. New York: Van Nostrand Reinhold, 1984.

Kharbanda, O. P. *Project Cost Control in Action*. Englewood Cliffs, N.J.: Prentice-Hall, 1981.

Kidder, T. *The Soul of a New Machine*. Boston: Little, Brown, 1981.

Lee, S. M., Moeller, G. L., and Digman, L. A. *Network Analysis for Management Decisions*. Boston: Kluwer Nijhoff, 1982.

Lock, D. *Project Management*. New York: St. Martin's Press, 1984.

Lustman, F. *Managing Computer Projects*. Reston, Va.: Reston Publishing, 1985.

Margin, O. C. *Project Management*. New York: AMACOM, 1976.

Markus, M. L. *Systems in Organizations: Bugs and Features*. Boston: Pitman, 1984.

Meland, S. *Electrical Project Management*. New York: McGraw-Hill, 1984.

Meredith, J. R., and Mantel, S. J. *Project Management: A Managerial Approach*. New York: Wiley, 1985.

Moder, J. J. *Project Management with CPM, PERT, and Precedence Diagramming*. New York: Van Nostrand Reinhold, 1983.

Murphy, K. J. *Macroproject Development in the Third World*. Boulder, Colo.: Westview Press, 1983.

Ouchi, W. G. *Theory Z: How American Business Can Meet the Japanese Challenge*. Reading, Mass.: Addison-Wesley, 1981.

Peddie, R. A. *The Management of Large High Technology Projects*. London: Central Electricity Generating Board, 1976.

Peters, T. J., and Waterman, R. H., Jr. *In Search of Excellence*. New York: Harper & Row, 1982.

Project Management Institute. *The Implementation of Project Management*. Reading, Mass.: Addison-Wesley, 1981.

Roman, D. D. *Managing Projects: A Systems Approach*. New York: Elsevier North-Holland, 1985.

Rosenau, M. D. *Successful Project Management*. Belmont, Calif.: Wadsworth, 1981.

Samaras, T. T. *Computerized Project Management Techniques for Manufacturing and Construction Industries*. Englewood Cliffs, N.J.: Prentice-Hall, 1979.

Sayles, L. R. *Managing Large Systems: Organizations for the Future*. New York: Harper & Row, 1971.

Shneiderman, B. *Software Psychology*. Boston: Little, Brown, 1980.

Silverman, M. *Project Management*. New York: Wiley, 1976.

Souder, W. E. *Project Selection and Economic Appraisal*. New York: Van Nostrand Reinhold, 1984.

Spinner, M. *Elements of Project Management*. Englewood Cliffs, N.J.: Prentice-Hall, 1981.

Staffurth, C. *Project Cost Control Using Networks*. London: Operational Research Society and Institute of Cost and Works Accountants, 1969.

Stock, R. *The Uses of Decision Theory in Public Programs and Project Management*. San Diego, Calif.: Institute of Public and Urban Affairs, San Diego State University, 1978.

Thomsett, R. *People and Project Management*. New York: Yourdon Press, 1980.

Turner, W. S. *Project Auditing Methodology*. New York: Elsevier North-Holland, 1980.

Weinberg, G. M. *The Psychology of Computer Programming*. New York: Van Nostrand Reinhold, 1971.

Wooldridge, S. *Project Management in Data Processing*. San Francisco: Petrocelli Books, 1976.

Yourdon, E. *Managing the Structured Techniques*. New York: Yourdon Press, 1979.

Zeldman, M. *Keeping Technical Projects on Target*. New York: AMACOM, 1978.

Index

A

Actual cost of work performed (ACWP), and earned value technique, 200–201, 204

Ambiguity: and application prototyping, 135; and conflict, 134; and flexibility, 133–134; in information-age projects, 134–135; and lack of expertise, 135–137; and language, 133; and oversights, 137–138

Amdahl, M., 104–106

Amdahl, R., 104–106, 112

"Appliance Masters," and flights of fancy, 140–141

Application prototyping: and ambiguity, 135; for requirements, 151–153

Aristotle, 35

Arthur Andersen & Co., and contracted projects, 211

Arthur D. Little, Inc., and contracted projects, 211

Arthur Young & Co., and contracted projects, 211

Authority: bureaucratic, 32–33; charismatic, 34; concept of, 30; formal, 31–32; nurturing, 30–35; purse-string, 32; responsibility divorced from, 17, 27–30; technical, 33–34

Auxiliary expenses, in budget, 178

B

Blanchard, K., 51

Block, M., 26, 27, 29

Block, R., 43, 226, 227

Boar, B., 153

Boss, in organizational environment, 37–38

Briggs, K. C., 62, 63

Bronfman, M., 139

Brooks, F. P., 95, 98

Budget: components of, 177–179; control of, 180–182; and cumulative cost curve, 182–183; and management reserve, 179–180

Budgeted cost of work performed (BCWP), and earned value technique, 200–202, 204

Budgeted cost of work scheduled (BCWS), and earned value technique, 200–204

Bureaucratic milestones, planning and control with, 217–220

C

Churchill, W., 43

Cleland, D. I., 127

Cohen, R., 53–54

Colleagues, in organizational environment, 38

Communication: and ambiguity of language, 133; channels of, 84–85; and doing right at first try, 59; as end, 84–85; and garbled messages, 86–87; and information clogging, 85–86; and misinterpretation, 147–148; and